DATE T4-ADQ-888

FEB 1 1 1976 DECKERVILLE	APR 1 3 1977	
JUN 1976 HARBOR BEACH		
SEP 0 8 1976 DRYDEN		
AUG 4 1976		
DEC 0 8 1976 YALE		

DEMCO 38-297

j616.994
B
    Berger, Melvin
      Cancer lab.

B75504

BLUE WATER LIBRARY FEDERATION
Headquarters: St. Clair County Library

CANCER LAB

SCIENTISTS AT WORK

CANCER LAB

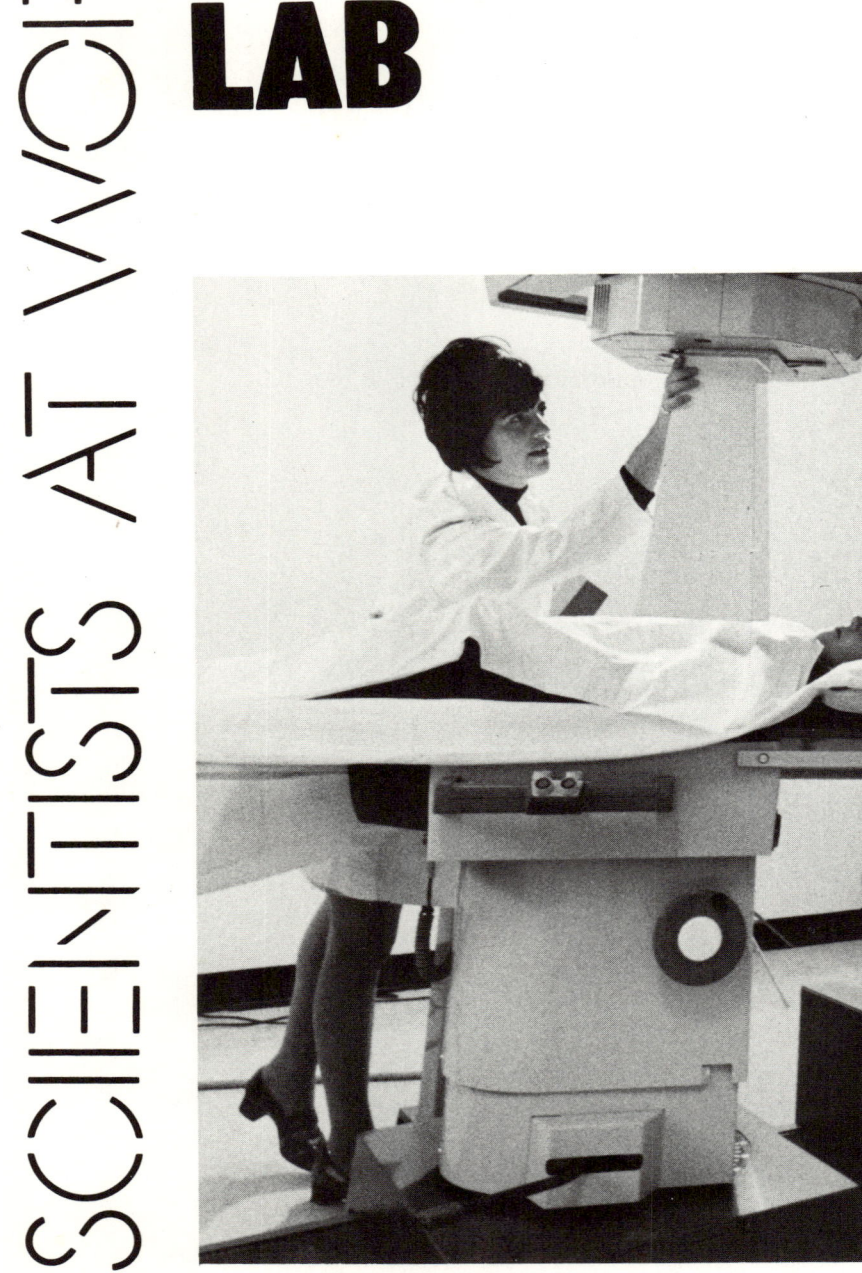

MELVIN BERGER

Foreword by
WILLIAM S. GRAY

Illustrated with photographs

THE JOHN DAY COMPANY
NEW YORK

Copyright © 1975 by Melvin Berger

Library of Congress Cataloging in Publication Data
Berger, Melvin.
   Cancer lab.
   (His Scientists at work)
   SUMMARY: An introduction to cancer, cancer research, and associated career opportunities. Discusses the particular activities of some leading scientists in their research laboratories.
   Bibliography: p.
   1. Cancer—Juvenile literature. [1. Cancer]
I. Title. [DNLM: 1. Laboratories—Juvenile literature.
2. Neoplasms—Prevention and control—Juvenile literature. 3. Research—Juvenile literature. QZ201 B496c]
RC263.B43   1974   616.9'94   74-9369

ISBN 0-381-99626-3 RB

All rights reserved. No part of this book may be reprinted, or reproduced or utilized in any form or by any electronic, mechanical or other means, now known or hereafter invented, including photocopying and recording, or in any information storage and retrieval system, without permission in writing from the Publisher.

Published simultaneously in Canada by
Fitzhenry & Whiteside Limited, Toronto.

Manufactured in the United States of America

Designed by Stanley S. Drate
1 2 3 4 5 6 7 8 9 10

This book is dedicated to
the memory of my mother,
who died of cancer
at too young an age.

BOOKS BY MELVIN BERGER

THOSE AMAZING COMPUTERS!
Uses of Modern Thinking Machines

In the SCIENTISTS AT WORK series

South Pole Station
The National Weather Service
Animal Hospital
Oceanography Lab
Pollution Lab
Cancer Lab

CONTENTS

ACKNOWLEDGMENTS	8
FOREWORD	10
CANCER: AN INTRODUCTION	13
THE PHYSICIAN	20
THE SURGEON	29
THE RADIOTHERAPIST	35
THE CHEMOTHERAPIST	46
THE IMMUNOLOGIST	53
CLINICAL LAB WORKERS	65
THE PATHOLOGIST	75
CANCER-CAUSE RESEARCHERS	85
THE VIROLOGISTS	95
DRUG SCREENERS	104
BASIC CANCER RESEARCHERS	113
FURTHER READING	123
INDEX	125

ACKNOWLEDGMENTS

This book could not have been written without the kind help of the scientists and staffs of several outstanding cancer research labs. The scientists invited me to visit their labs, to observe and photograph them at work, and to discuss their research with them. The staff members made all the arrangements for my visits, and furnished me with many of the photographs that appear in the book.

Among the many scientists and staff members to whom I want to express my gratitude, there are a few I would like to single out for special words of appreciation. At the National Cancer Institute: Mr. William S. Gray, Mrs. Margaret L. Layton, and Drs. George P. Canellos, Richard

Fisher, Jonathan L. Hartwell, John B. Moloney, Joseph Robinson and David Sachs. At Memorial Sloan-Kettering Cancer Center: Dr. Martin Fleischer, Mr. Sammie Jackson, and Ms. Adele Slocum. At the Cold Spring Harbor Laboratory: Dr. Raymond Gesteland.

At the Nassau County Medical Center: Drs. John O. Archembeau and David Lubell, and Mr. Michael De Luca. At the American Cancer Society: Ms. Adele Paroni. Dr. Robert E. Perdue of the Department of Agriculture, Dr. Leo Gross of the Waldemar Medical Research Foundation, Dr. E. A. Mirand of the Roswell Park Memorial Institute, and Mr. Stern and Ms. Farenthold of the National Institutes of Health.

FOREWORD

I am particularly pleased to be asked to help in the preparation of this book by Mr. Berger and add a few words of introduction. My own interest in cancer began in the eighth grade when a neighbor, who had left medical school to fight in World War II, lent me his Zeiss microscope. I built a tiny lab next to my father's bed, and there, for long hours in the night, when I was supposed to be studying math and Latin, I peered through those magnificent German lenses into the world 1,000 times smaller than the eye can see. The shapes and colors of cells and bacteria, and my brother's fishbait earthworm, fascinated me so much that I knew someday I would become a doctor or pathologist.

I never became one, because I had my own war to fight and college science was harder than Latin or math. But in that strange way that fate or God moves us all with a purpose which we may not recognize, I have become as much a part of the war on cancer as the doctors with whom I now work.

In 1967, I was dying of hopelessly advanced Hodgkin's disease. I was ineffectually treated by private physicians who finally abandoned me at the doorsteps of the National Cancer Institute.

Stripped of health, confidence, financial resources, and on the verge of death, I entered the largest medical research complex in the world, sustained only by an abiding faith and hope that these Federal doctors who labor long for small wages might abrogate my sentence of death.

My human need was filled and my faith was sustained by these tireless dedicated men. My cancer has been cured and it is my deepest hope that every human stricken with cancer may share my good fortune.

Dr. Vincent De Vita, and the other National Cancer Institute doctors, nurses and technicians about whom you will read in this book command admiration, love and respect.

But for you young men and women who read this book, I would like to say this. It is probable that the enormous burden of cancer will be lifted forever from the shoulders of mankind in your lifetime. But if this is to come to pass, the brilliant ideas from which this human victory will be built must come from you. The journey has only begun. You will carry us forward, and at the end it will probably be said of you that in conquering cancer your generation has unlocked also the ultimate riddles of life and aging.

> WILLIAM S. GRAY
> *Chief, Education and Technical Reports Branch*
> *National Cancer Institute*
> *Bethesda, Maryland*

CANCER: AN INTRODUCTION

Right now, thousands of scientists are waging an all-out war against cancer. Armed with millions of dollars of equipment and support, they are doing research in hundreds of laboratories and hospitals all over the country. Each one is a soldier in the army of workers who want to rid people of this terrible disease.

There is much that cancer scientists need to find out about cancer. But there is a great deal that they already know.

Research has shown that cancer is not one disease. It is a group of more than 100 different diseases. Each one may develop in different parts of the body, such as the lung, the stomach, the skin and so on.

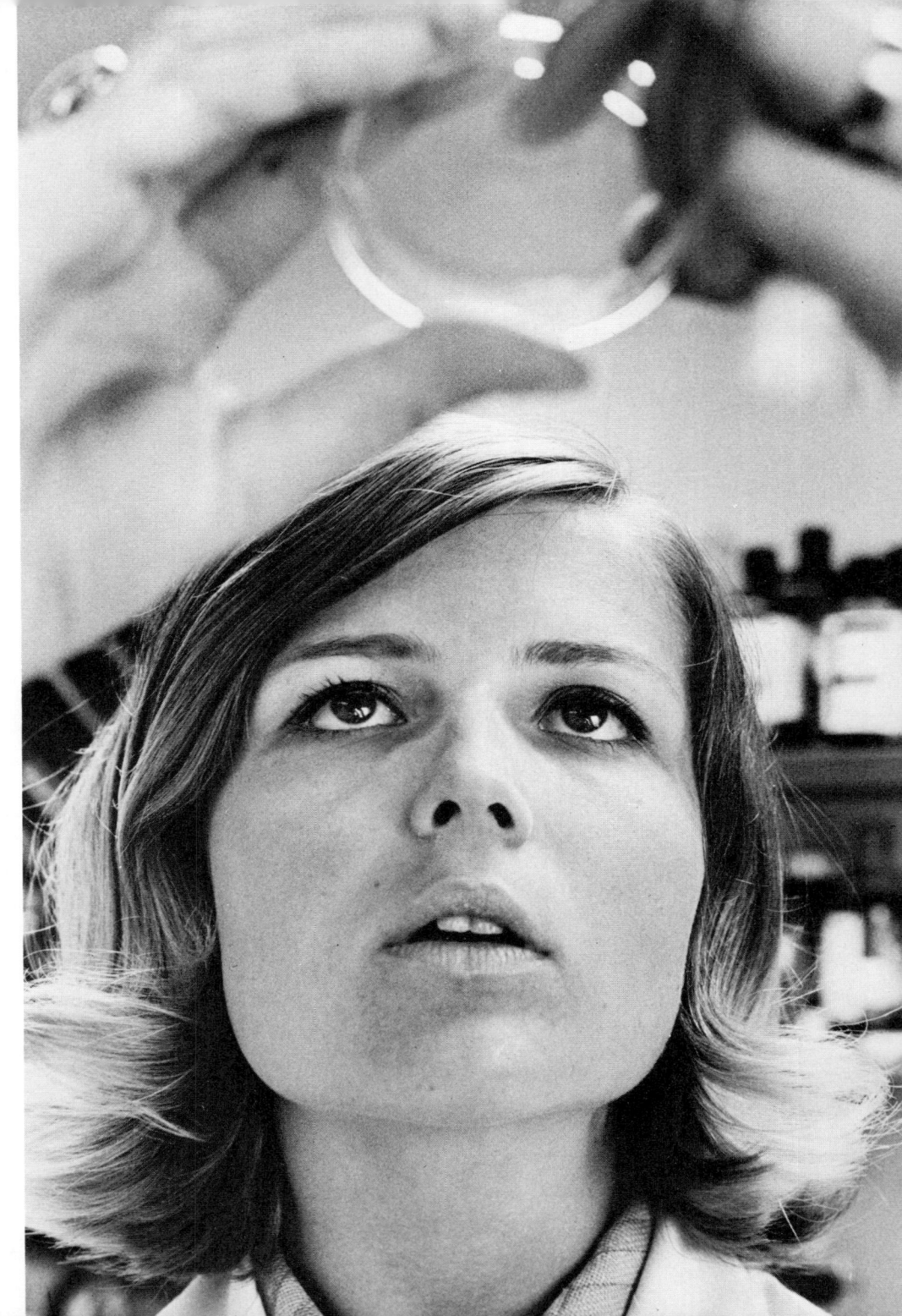

Cancer scientists do not expect to find a single cure for all these diseases. They are looking for different cures for the different cancers. A "cure" for cancer is a treatment that allows the patient to live a normal lifespan free of the disease. Over one million people in the United States have survived ten, twenty or more years after treatment.

Scientists also know that cancer is a disease of the cells. All living beings are made up of tiny units called cells. There are billions and billions of cells in the human body. Normally, these cells live, grow and divide in an orderly, controlled way.

Sometimes, though, some of these cells start to grow in a wild, uncontrolled way. They crowd out normal cells. They are called cancer cells. Each time a cancer cell divides to form new cells, the new cells are cancer cells, too.

The cancer cells keep on growing and dividing until there are so many cancer cells that they form a lump, or cancer.

The cancer pushes and crowds the nearby normal cells, robbing them of food and interfering with the functions of healthy tissues and organs. Sometimes cells break away from the original cancer and are carried to other parts of the body. New cancers develop. This causes additional damage to healthy parts of the body. If the cancer growth is not stopped, the patient eventually dies.

Until recently, there was almost no hope for cancer patients. Today, one out of three cancer victims can be saved, if the disease is detected and treated promptly.

Early detection is one of the most important goals of cancer researchers. With new and better ways to detect cancer, they hope to be able to save even more lives.

Thousands of scientists are now doing cancer research. This young scientist is trying to learn more about the causes of cancer.
PHOTO: MEMORIAL SLOAN-KETTERING CANCER CENTER

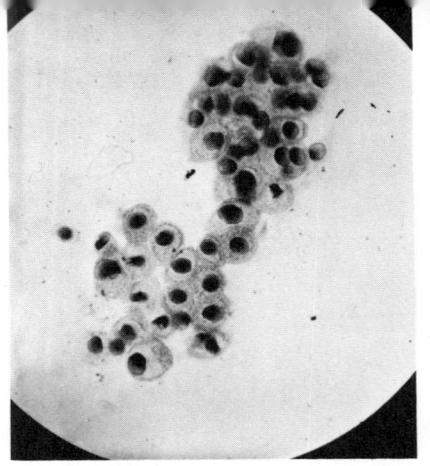 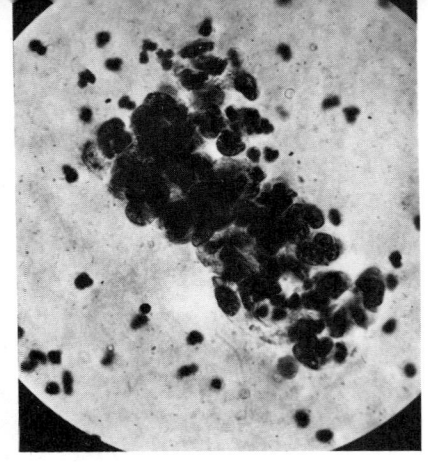

Normal cells (left) and cancer cells (right) look very different when seen through a microscope.

One of three cancer patients can be saved if the disease is detected early and treated promptly.
PHOTO: NASSAU COUNTY MEDICAL CENTER

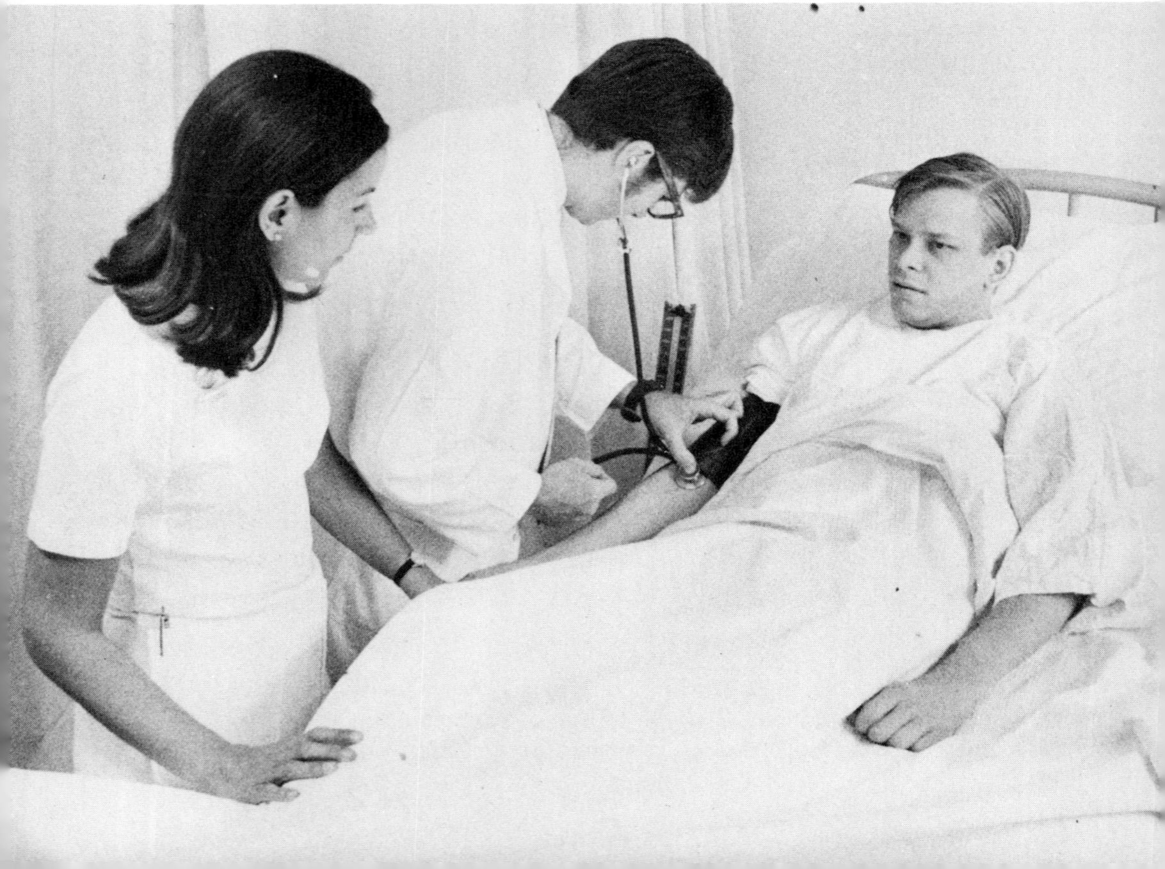

The scientist's lab bench is filled with equipment as he does research into the basic science of cancer.
PHOTO: NATIONAL INSTITUTES OF HEALTH

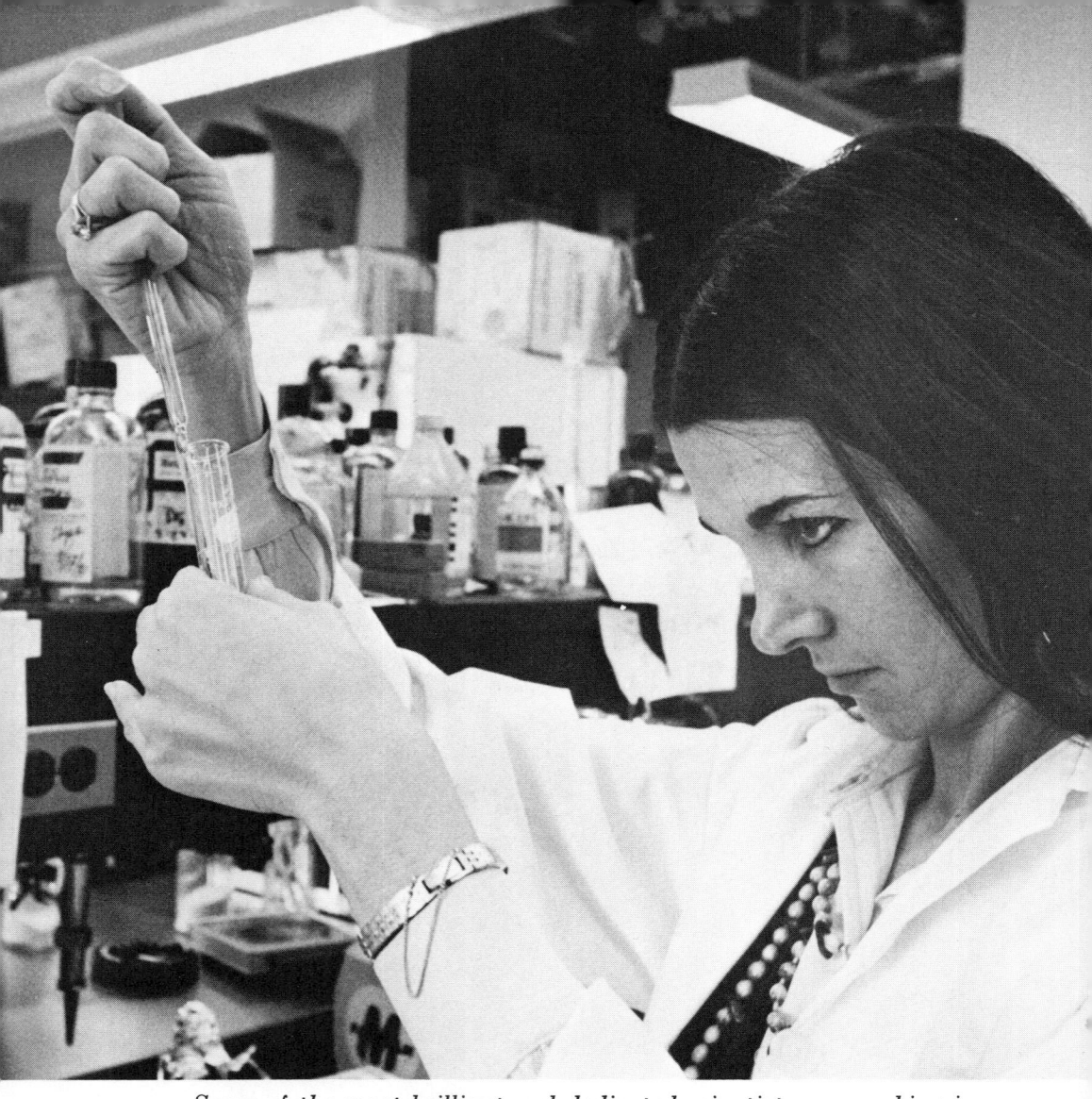
Some of the most brilliant and dedicated scientists are working in cancer research. Here the scientist is growing cells in a test tube.
PHOTO: NATIONAL INSTITUTES OF HEALTH

There is also a search for better ways to treat the disease, once it is detected. Some cancer scientists develop and test new drugs and methods of treatment. Others perform tests on blood and tissue samples taken from patients. Their tests and studies help physicians plan the best treatment for each patient.

Other scientists perform experiments to discover the causes of cancer. They observe the effects of different agents on cancer growth. They try to learn more about the connection between viruses and cancer. They test thousands of plants and chemicals to see if any will stop the growth of a cancer.

Finally, there are scientists who work to increase our basic understanding of the human cell. They gather information about the normal cell, so that they can better understand the cancer cell. Their discoveries help those who seek ways to detect, treat and prevent cancer.

The cancer researchers include some of the most brilliant and dedicated scientists of our time. They are gaining knowledge and understanding in their struggle to solve the mystery of cancer. Although cancer does not give up its secrets easily, the researchers are most hopeful.

Many cancer scientists predict that they will learn how to prevent, cure or control all cancers within your lifetime. The researchers in today's labs are moving toward one of the most important medical achievements of all time—the conquest of cancer!

THE PHYSICIAN

The physician is giving the patient her regular annual checkup. She looks into her ears, mouth and throat. She checks her eyes and listens to her heart. She asks questions about her general health.

The physician is looking for symptoms of disease. Her four years of premedical college training, four years in medical school and two or more years as an intern or resident in a hospital, have taught her to recognize the symptoms of most diseases.

As part of the examination, the physician asks, "Do you have a lump anywhere in your body? Do you have a sore that doesn't heal? Any difficulty in swallowing? Any bleed-

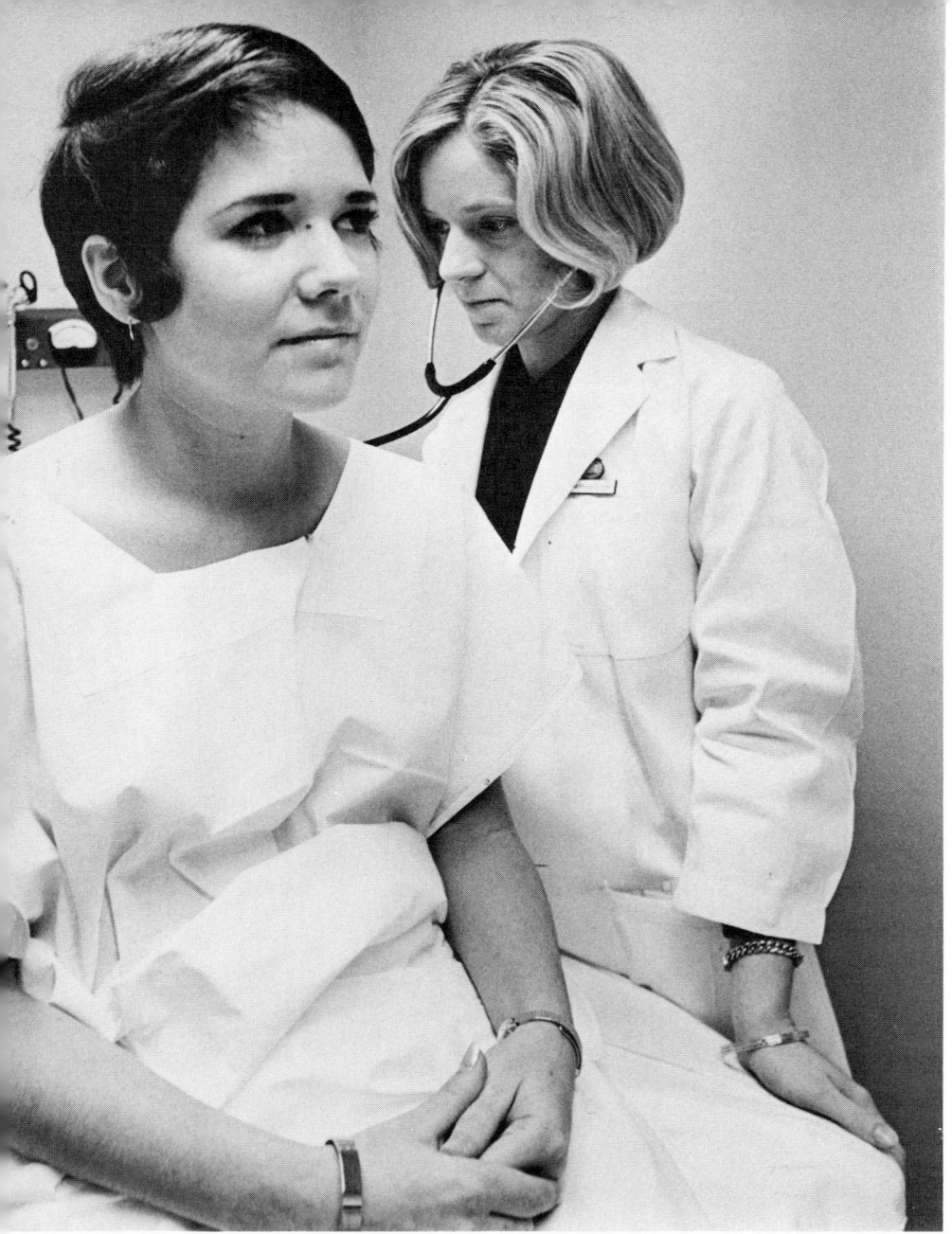

The physician listens to the patient's heart with her stethoscope.
PHOTO: NATIONAL INSTITUTES OF HEALTH

ing? A cough that doesn't go away? Any persistent or unusual pains? Have you had a sustained loss of weight? Have you had any unexplained fevers? Have any of these symptoms lasted for several weeks?"

Any of these symptoms *might* be a signal of cancer. The same symptoms, though, are also caused by many other diseases. It is up to the physician to make the right diagnosis.

The physician touches and feels the patient's neck and some other areas. She looks for any unusual growths or lumps that the patient may not have noticed. Not every lump, of course, is cancer. Most lumps are harmless growths, called benign tumors. Only lumps that keep growing and spreading are dangerous. They are called malignant tumors, or cancers.

Physicians cannot feel many of the cancers that grow inside the body. They use different methods to detect these types of cancers.

The physicians may look at cells collected from various organs inside the body. They can tell if a cancer is present by examining the cells under a microscope.

The well-known Pap test (first instituted by Dr. George Papanicolaou) works this way. It is one of the most reliable ways for physicians to detect cancer of the uterus (or womb), a part of the reproductive system in women. The doctor rubs a swab along the lining of the vagina (also part of the female reproductive system), the opening of the uterus, or in the uterus, to collect some cells for examination under a microscope. Abnormalities in the shape and structure of the cells indicate whether the patient has uterine cancer or perhaps a precancerous condition.

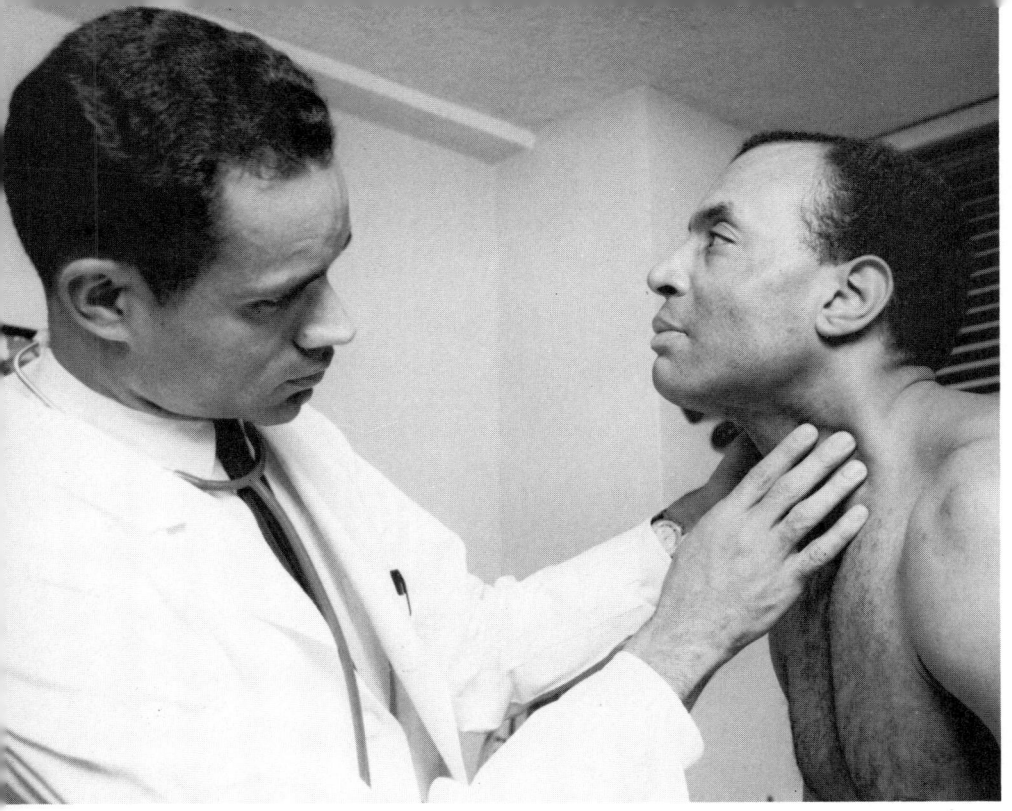

The physician carefully feels around the patient's neck for any signs of cancer. PHOTO: BERNARD LAWRENCE

Some physicians are doing experiments on the cells found in the material that people cough up. They hope to find cells here which will tell them whether the person has lung cancer or is in danger of developing it. Physicians are also looking for chemicals found only in the blood of people ill with cancer. This may prove to be a quick, easy way to catch other types of cancer at an early stage.

X rays are used to detect some of the cancers that form solid lumps within the body. These lumps block the X rays that pass through the normal tissues in the body.

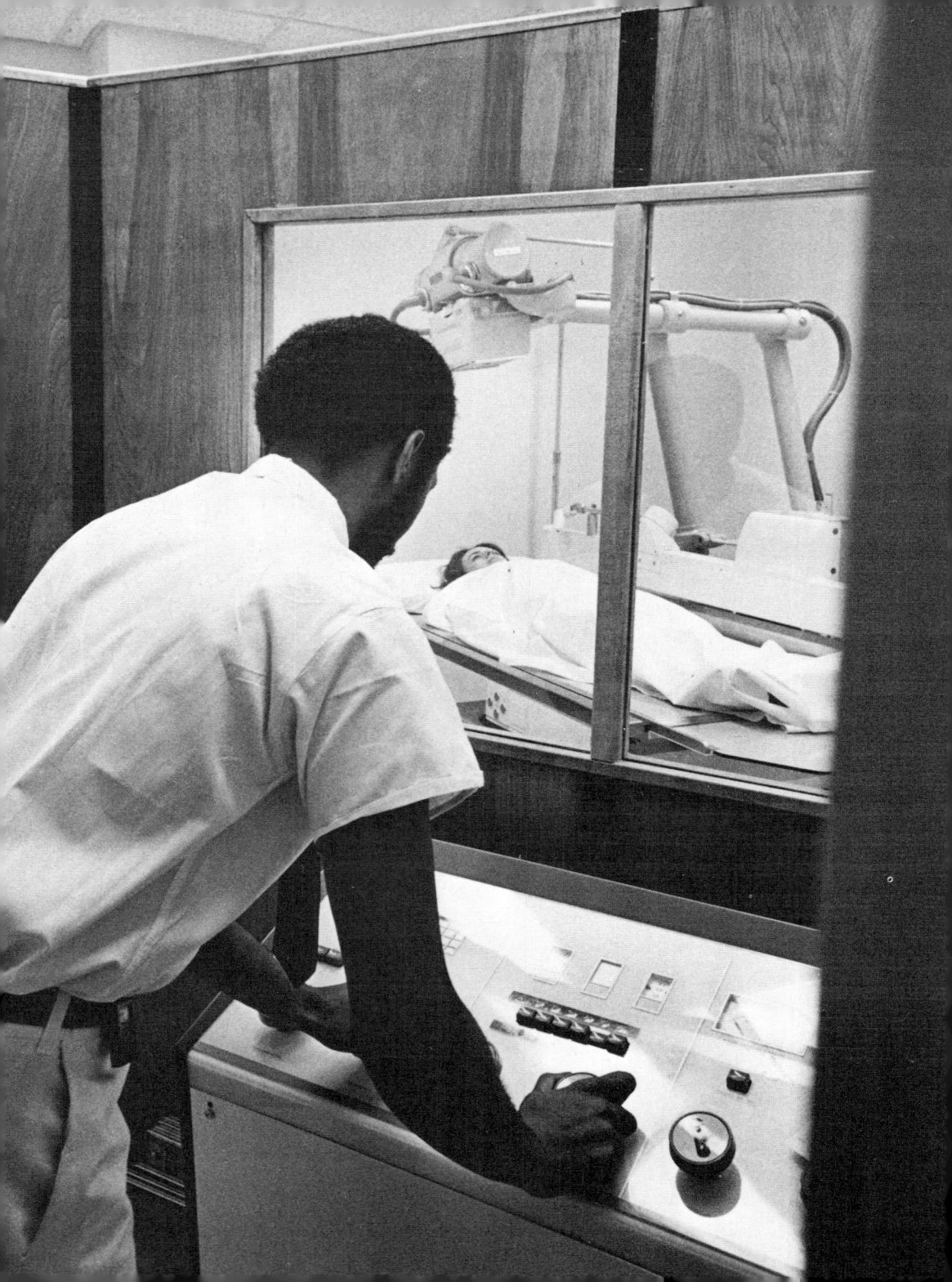

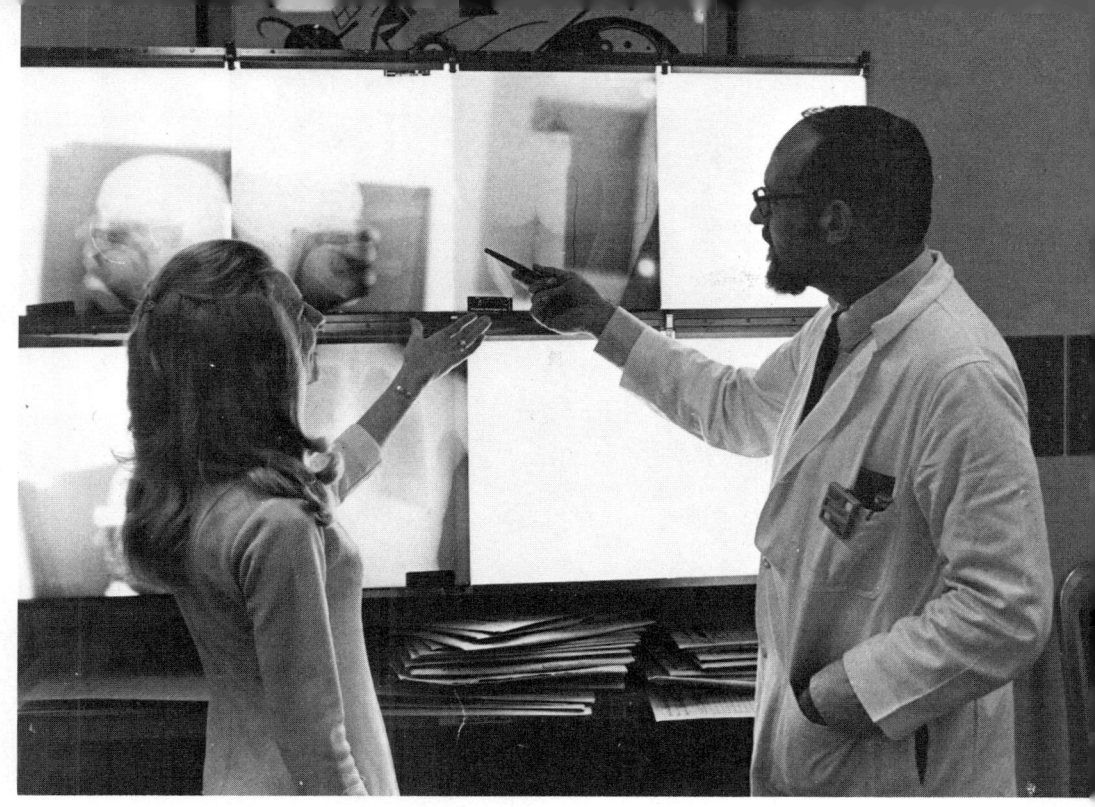

Two physicians study the X rays taken of a patient who might have a cancer growth. PHOTO: NASSAU COUNTY MEDICAL CENTER

If there is a cancer lump, the physician sees a shadow on the X-ray picture. The size, shape and location of the shadow help the physician decide if the growth is a cancer.

If the physician suspects cancer of the stomach, the patient may be given a special drink. This drink contains barium, a substance that blocks X rays. The physician then watches the patient through an X-ray viewing device, called a fluoroscope. The screen of the fluoroscope shows the barium moving through the patient's stomach. Anything blocking the stomach, like a cancer lump, is outlined by the barium.

The physician uses X rays to search for cancers within the body.
PHOTO: MEMORIAL SLOAN-KETTERING CANCER CENTER

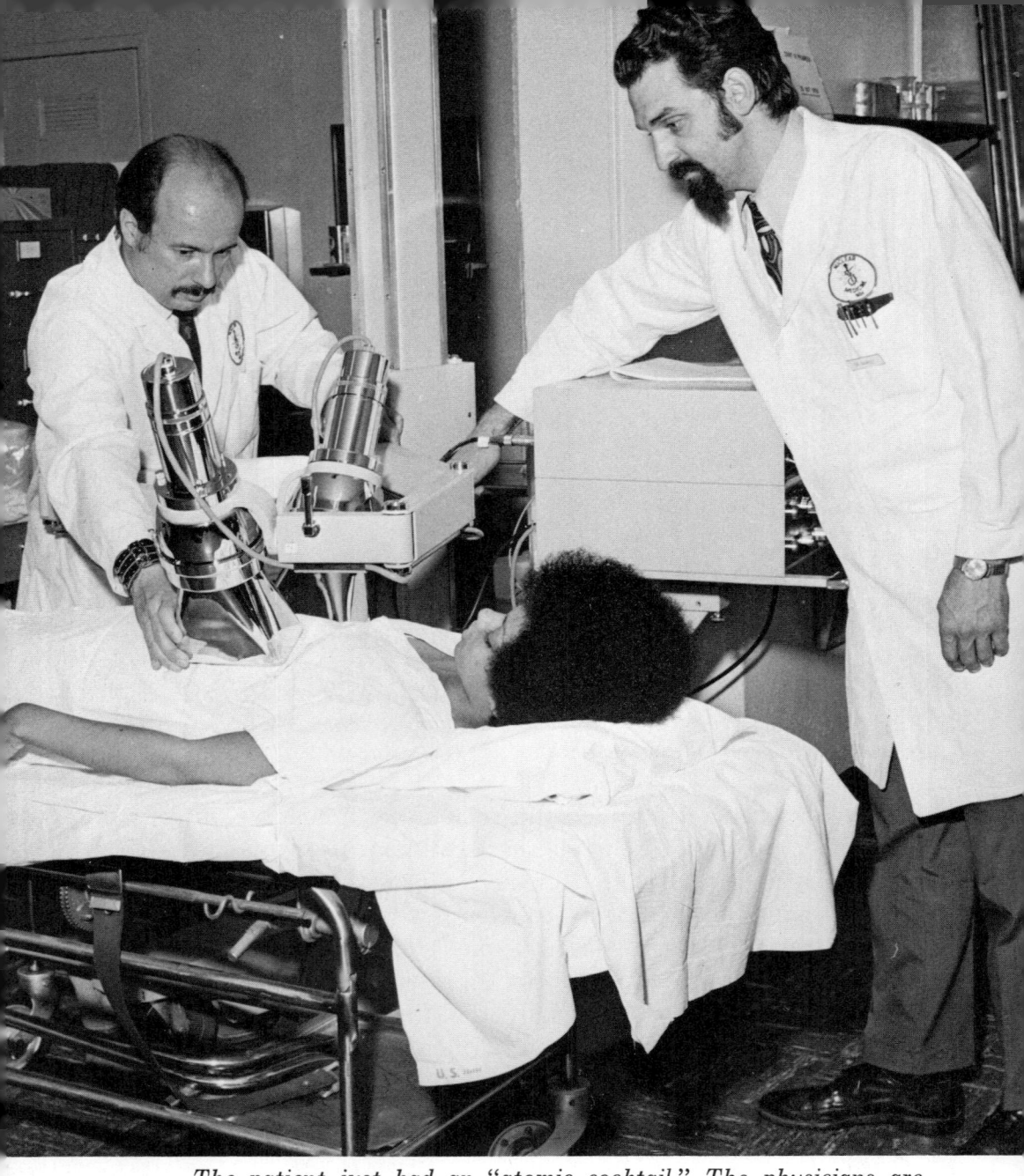
The patient just had an "atomic cocktail." The physicians are using the shiny metal scanner to trace its path in her body.
PHOTO: NATIONAL INSTITUTES OF HEALTH CLINICAL CENTER

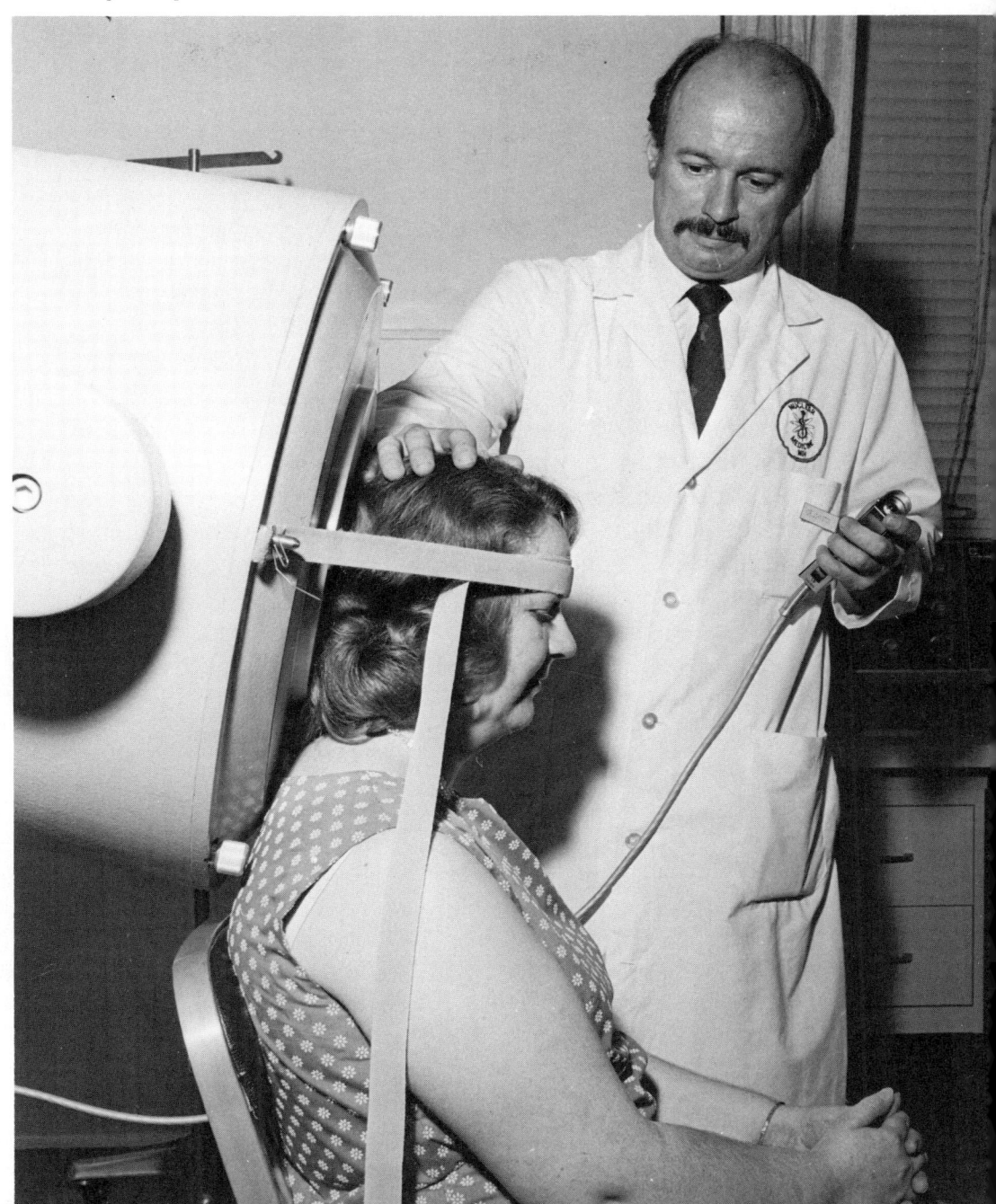

The scientist is using a giant camera behind the patient's head to take a picture of the flow of blood through her brain. A radioisotope in her blood sends out invisible rays that the special camera can pick up. PHOTO: NATIONAL INSTITUTES OF HEALTH CLINICAL CENTER

Sometimes the physician asks the patient to drink an "atomic cocktail." This drink contains a radioisotope. Radioisotopes are chemicals that are radioactive. They are always sending out invisible rays and tiny particles that are able to pass through most matter.

The radioisotope in the atomic cocktail is carefully chosen. It is one that will be attracted to cancer cells of the type the physician suspects might be present. After giving the patient the atomic cocktail, the physician moves a scanner over the patient's body. The scanner is an instrument that shows where the radioisotope has gone.

The radioactivity of the atomic cocktail is like a bell that is hung on a cat. You know where the cat is by listening for the bell. In the same way, the physician follows the radioisotope by tracing the radioactivity with a scanner as the radioisotope moves through the body.

Did the radioisotope all go to one spot? A cancer might be located there. How much radioactivity is there in that one place? The more radioactivity, the more cancer cells and the larger the cancer.

At times, the physician can make a fast, sure diagnosis of cancer based on the examination. Usually, though, the examination is not enough. The physician needs more information and turns to another doctor, the surgeon, for help.

THE SURGEON

A physician who suspects that a patient has cancer in some part of the body will often refer the patient to a surgeon. A surgeon is a medical doctor who performs operations to remove or repair tissues and organs in a patient's body. The surgeon has the same basic early training as other physicians, but with special training in surgery.

The surgeon usually admits the patient to a hospital. The only way to be sure that a growth is cancerous is to remove some of the suspicious tissue and examine it under a microscope. This frequently minor operation is called a biopsy.

The patient is taken to the operating room and is given

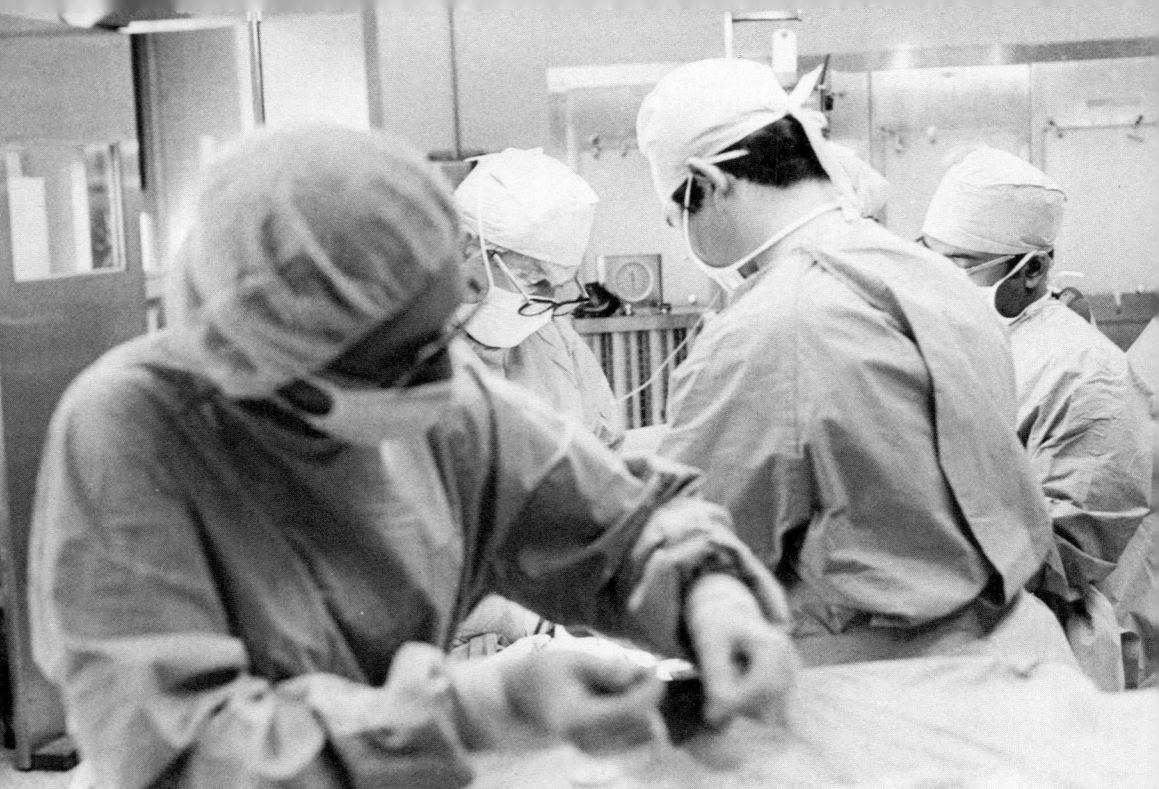

A biopsy is a very minor operation. But it is usually done in an operating room, with the surgeons wearing gowns and masks to prevent infection.
PHOTO: MEMORIAL SLOAN-KETTERING CANCER CENTER

an anesthetic, so that the person feels nothing during the operation. Then the surgeon removes a small bit of tissue from the growth. The specimen is immediately sent to the laboratory. It is examined under a microscope to see if it contains cancer cells.

If the specimen is benign (not cancerous), no further surgery may be necessary. The surgeon closes up the cut that was made, and the operation is over.

If there is cancer present, the surgeon may decide to remove the growth and sometimes additional surrounding tissues. In most cases where the cancer has not spread, the best treatment is to remove it by surgery. Surgery is used in about three out of every four cancer cases.

During the operation, the surgeon looks carefully to see if the cancer has spread. If it has, the decision may be made to remove nearby tissue or glands as well. The most important thing is to remove every cancer cell. Any that are left in the body are likely to start growing again.

At the same time, the surgeon tries to remove the least possible amount of tissue. The body needs every organ, gland, bone, blood vessel and muscle it contains. The surgeon wants to take out every cancer cell without harming any vital part of the body.

Surgeons and other researchers are always working to improve surgery as a treatment for cancer. In the past, the surgeons had difficult decisions to make in many cancer operations. Should they remove every bit of tissue where there might be cancer cells? If they did, the patient might be badly disfigured or might not survive the surgery. Should they take a chance and leave tissue which might contain cancer cells? If they did, cancer might strike again.

Now surgeons frequently operate to remove all of the cancer. They use special new drugs before and during surgery. These drugs shrink the size of the cancer, build up the patients' strength and protect them against infection.

Physicians are now able to furnish better care after

surgery. More and more patients are surviving major operations in which important organs and entire parts of the body are removed.

Cancer researchers have found ways to speed up the patient's recovery. There is physical therapy to help build up the patient's body. There are devices, such as artificial limbs for instance, to help the patient's appearance.

Another new approach in cancer surgery is organ transplants. In some cases the growing cancer is destroying a vital organ. The only hope may be to replace the damaged organ with a healthy organ transplant.

The surgeons study X rays of the cancer growth before starting an operation. PHOTO: MEMORIAL SLOAN-KETTERING CANCER CENTER

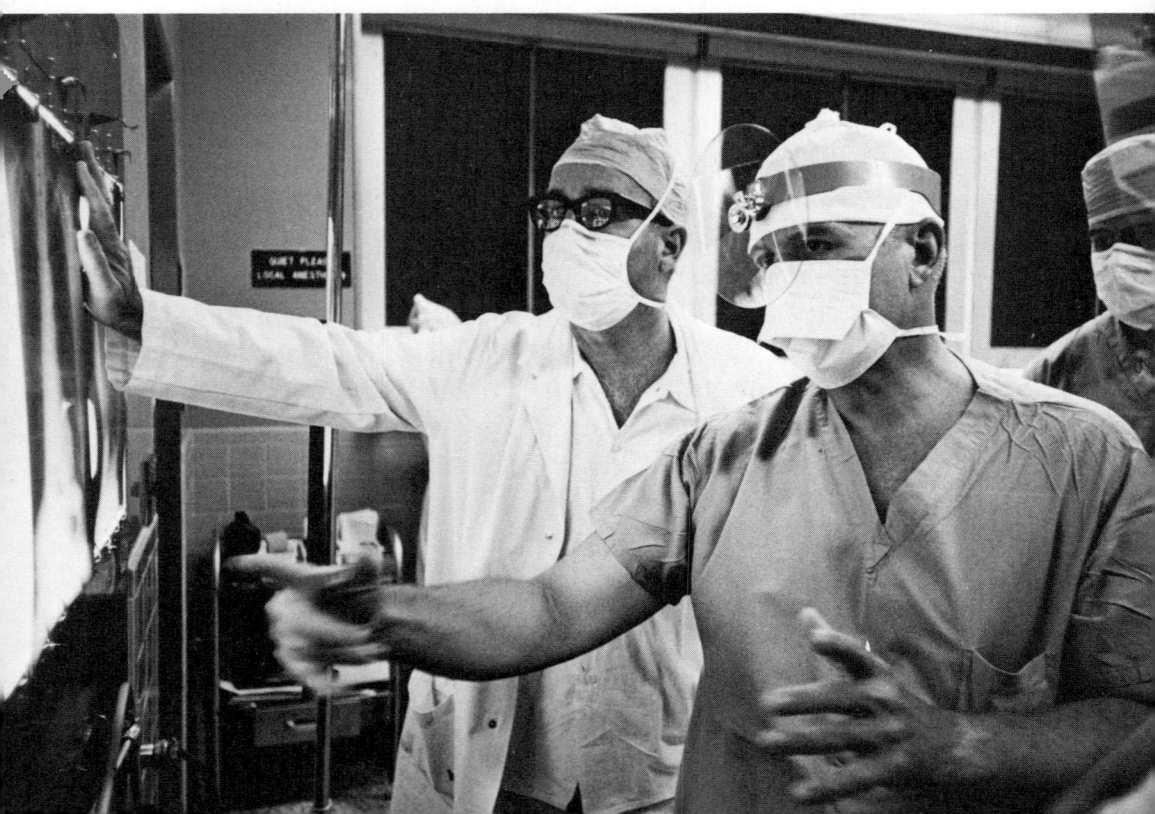

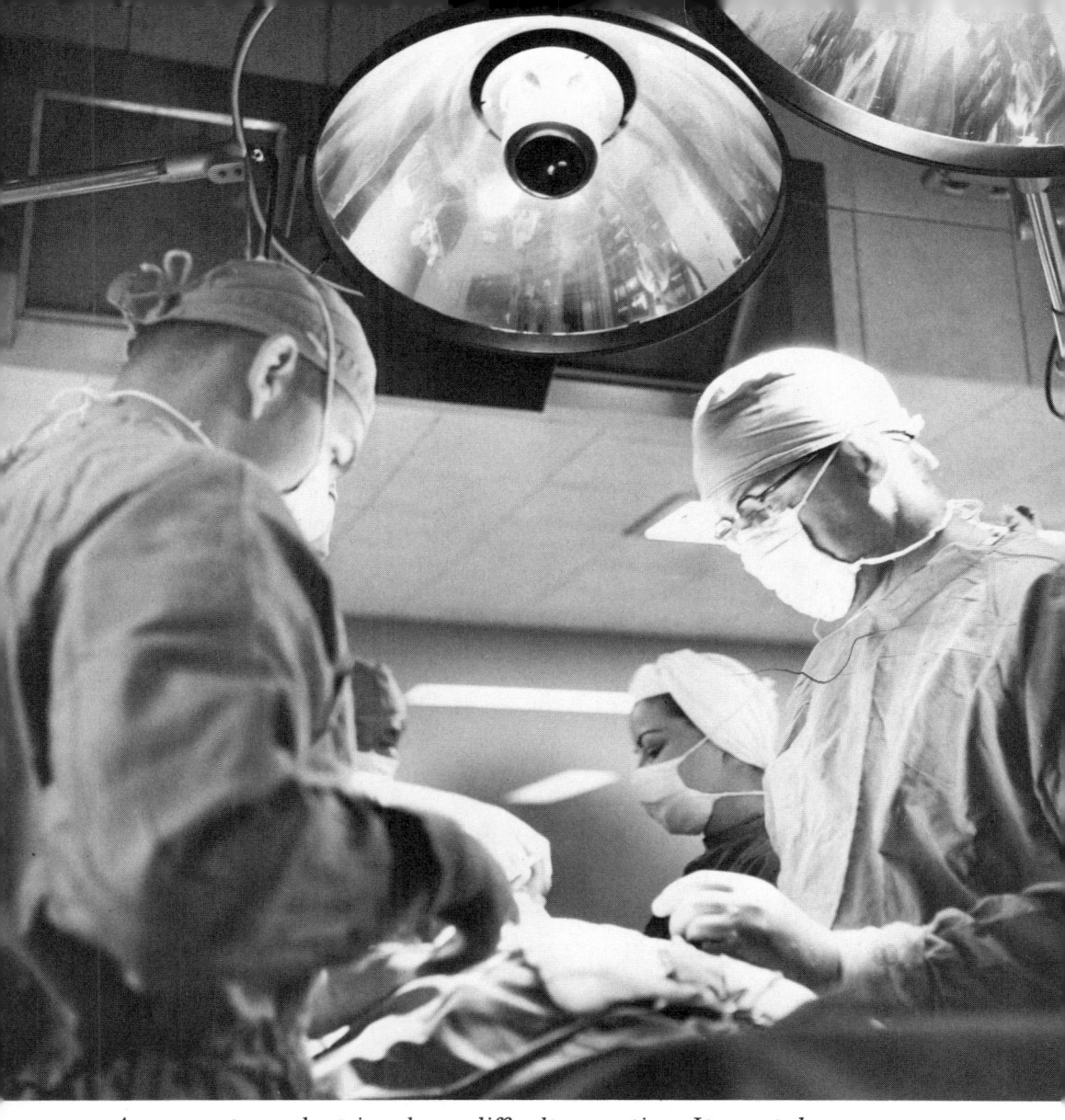

An organ transplant is a long, difficult operation. It can take several surgeons many hours to perform. PHOTO: ARTHUR LEIPZIG

An organ transplant is a long, difficult operation. It requires a team of highly skilled surgeons, physicians, nurses and technicians. One of the first transplants in a cancer patient, a liver transplant in 1972, took fourteen hours to complete.

The major medical problem in transplants is to make sure that the new organ is able to grow and do its job in the patient's body. The body's defense system treats the organ as an invader. It works to get rid of the invader, just as it fights germs that invade the body.

Surgeons have drugs that prevent the body from rejecting a new organ. These drugs knock out the body's defense system. But this may cause other troubles. The patient has no defense against any disease-causing germs that might enter the body. The result can be a successful transplant, but a seriously ill patient.

Cryosurgery, or surgery with cold, is used to destroy certain cancers by freezing them. The surgeon uses a blunt metal probe, cooled to a temperature of nearly 200 degrees below zero. As soon as the probe touches the diseased tissue, the cancer cells are immediately destroyed.

Cryosurgery is better than the usual surgery in treating some types of cancer. It is painless. There is no bleeding. And there is much less danger of scattering cancer cells during the operation.

The cancer surgeons today are using these, and several other new methods and tools, in their work. The latest advances in surgical research, in the hands of these skillful physicians, are helping to save the lives of many victims of cancer.

THE RADIOTHERAPIST

One physician in the cancer center is drawing different shapes, patterns and lines on a paper. From time to time, the physician checks figures on the computer. The computer has all the patients' records in its memory.

This physician is a radiotherapist. He has special training in the use of radiation to treat disease. He is qualified to administer radiation treatments to cancer patients. More than one-half of all cancer patients receive radiation treatment. Radiation is often used along with surgery and the other methods of treatment.

Radiation is the release of energy from an object. The light and heat from the sun are examples of radiation

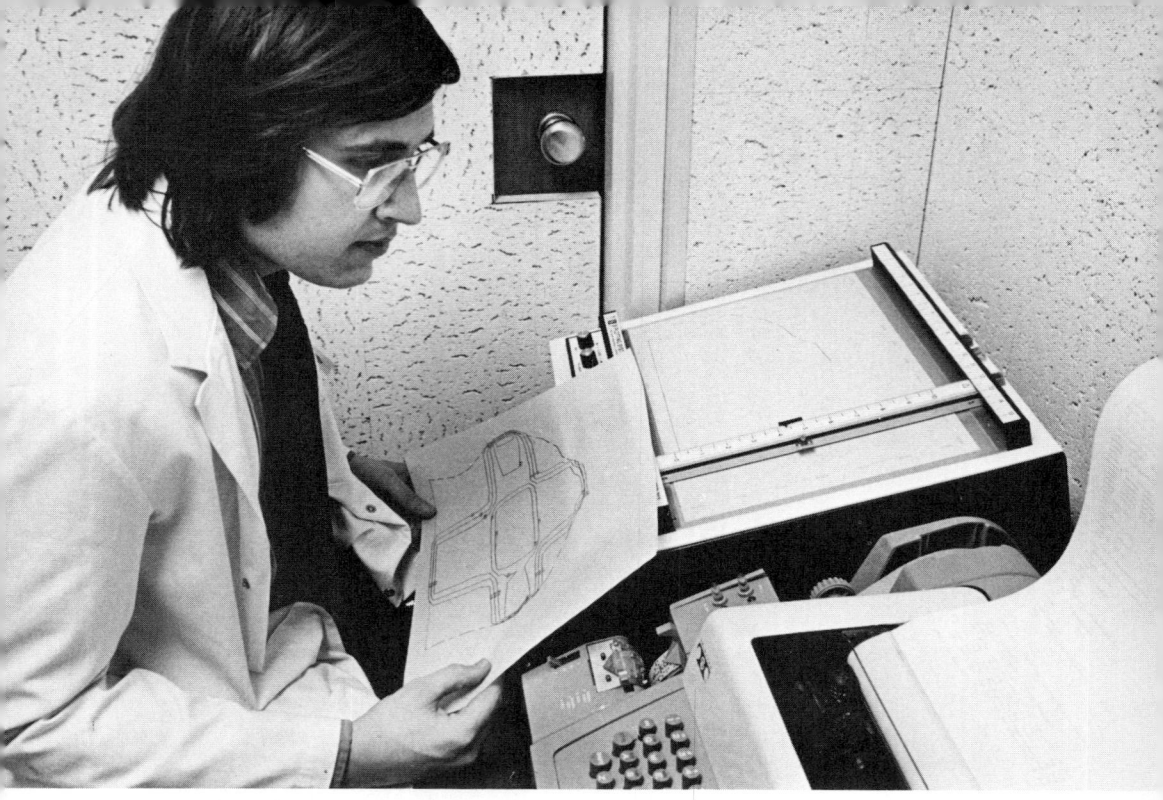

The physician checks the figures coming from a computer as he draws a diagram to plan a patient's radiation treatment.
PHOTO: MEMORIAL SLOAN-KETTERING CANCER CENTER

energy. But the radiotherapists use very special forms of radiation. They mostly use X rays and gamma rays. These rays are similar to light and heat radiation. But they have much shorter wave lengths. You cannot see or feel X rays or gamma rays. And they are able to pass through many solid substances, such as human flesh.

Scientists have known for a long time that radiation kills cells. More recently, they found out that radiation can kill cancer cells more easily than normal cells, and began to treat many cancers with radiation.

Since radiation can pass through flesh, it can be used to treat cancers anywhere in the body. Radiation is the best treatment for certain localized cancers, such as early Hodgkin's disease. It is also used to treat cancers that are so large that they cannot be removed, without badly damaging healthy tissue and organs, as well as for brain cancers and others which the surgeon cannot easily reach.

After a surgeon operates to remove a cancer, the patient is often given radiation treatment. The radiotherapist hopes to destroy, by radiation, any cells that were not removed by the surgeon.

The X-ray machine is the chief tool of the radiotherapist. The electrical circuit inside the machine creates the X rays. The machine is lined with lead to stop the X rays from escaping in all directions. The rays are beamed out through an opening in the lead. The radiotherapist controls the X-ray beam by changing the size and shape of the opening.

The latest research in X-ray therapy is on the use of high-energy X rays. Radiotherapists use very high voltages to produce the X rays. Some of the most modern X-ray machines use a betatron or a linear accelerator, to get high-energy X rays. In these devices, electrons are made to move faster and faster. They are then flung against a metal target that produces the powerful X rays. The early results show that high-energy X rays can be aimed more exactly at the cancer, and cause less damage to healthy tissue.

Cobalt-60 is a very popular source of radiation. It is an element that is made radioactive in a nuclear reactor. It then gives off gamma rays, a form of radiation similar to

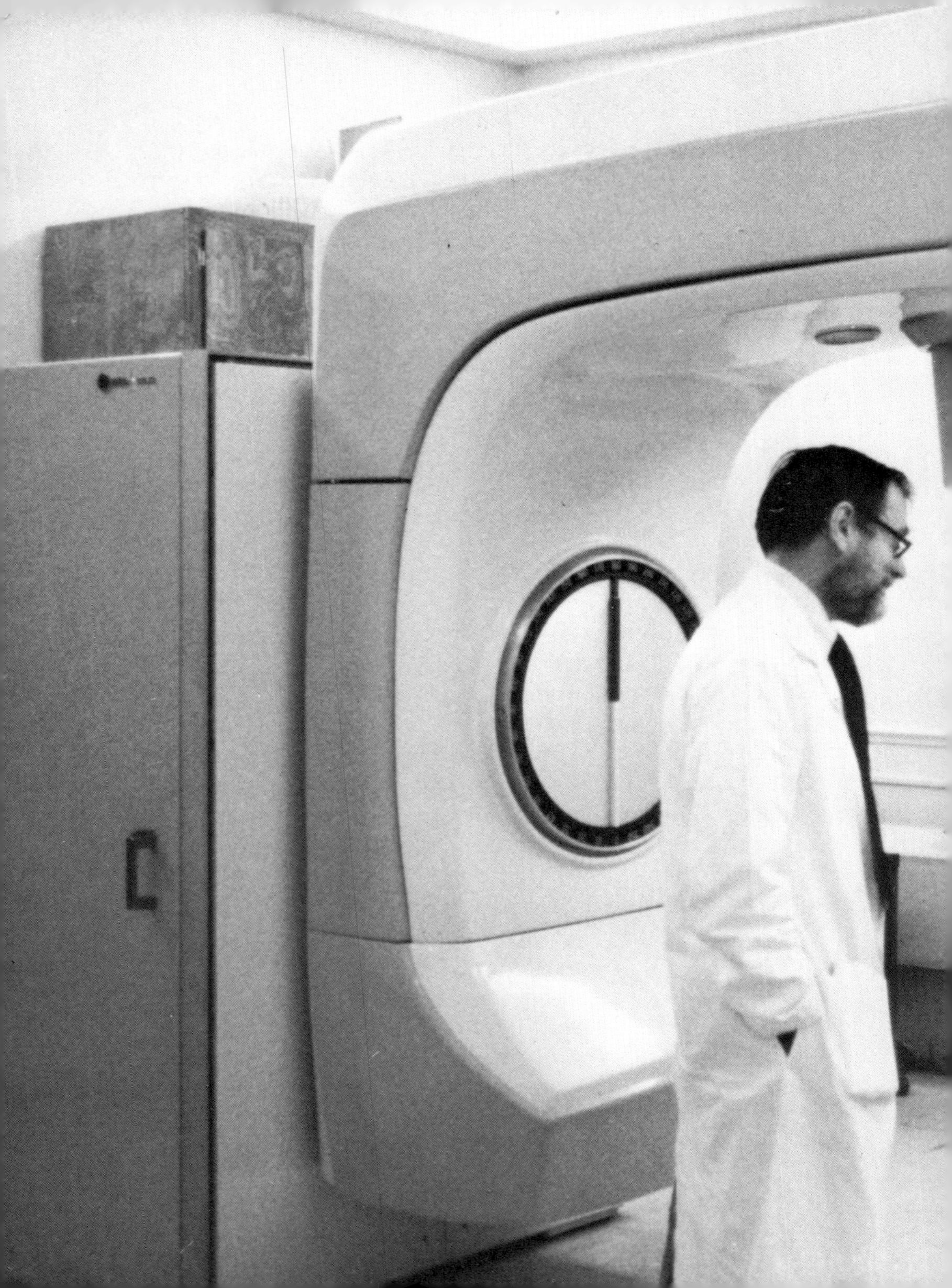

Radiotherapist Dr. John O. Archambeau watches a patient under a high-energy X-ray machine. During the treatment, invisible X rays are beamed at the cancer growth.
PHOTO: NASSAU COUNTY MEDICAL CENTER

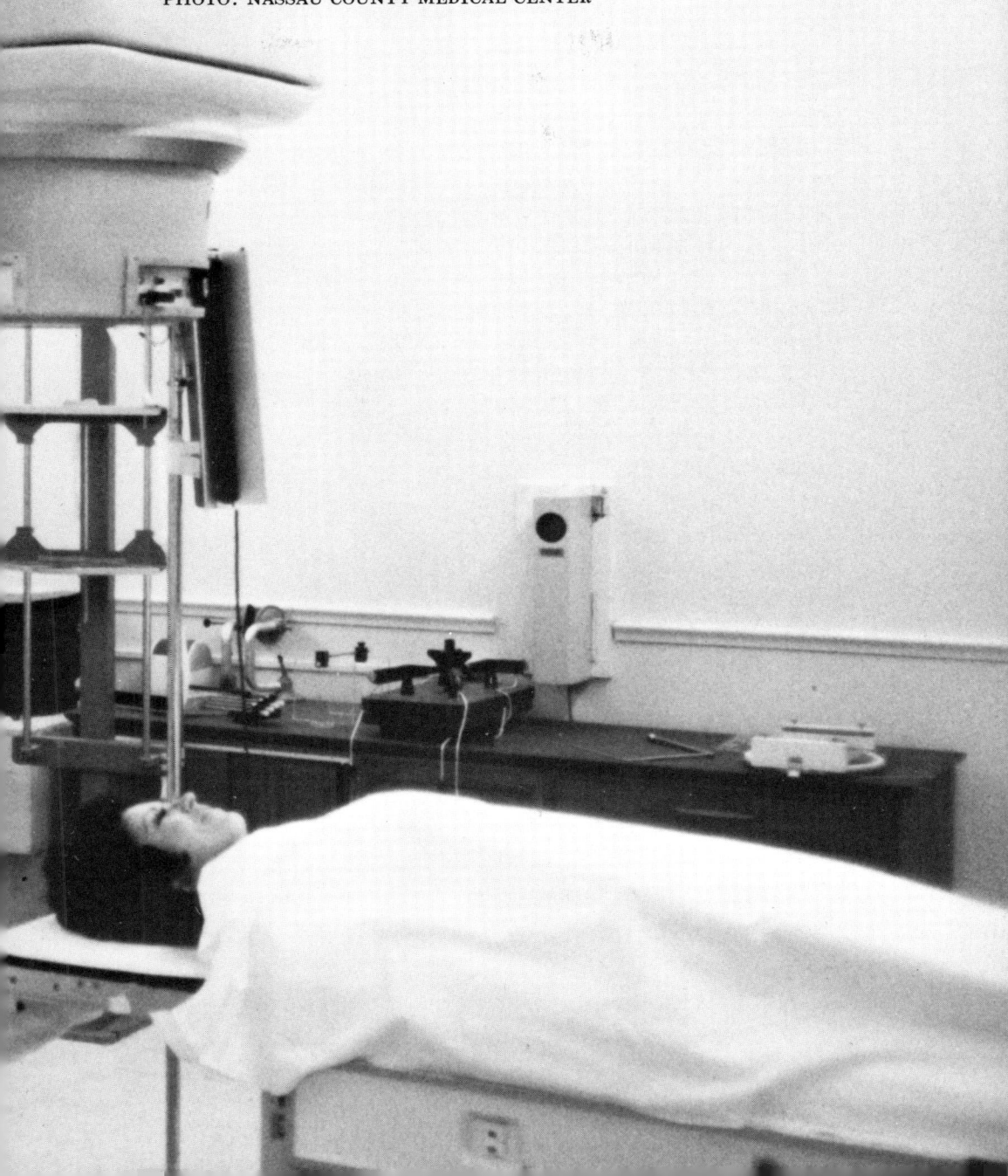

X rays. A "slug" of cobalt-60 is placed in the head of the machine. The gamma rays given off by the cobalt are so powerful that the lead lining to contain the rays is one foot thick!

Working with the patient's own physician, the radiotherapist plans the radiation treatment. He decides whether to use X rays or cobalt-60; how much of the patient's body to expose to the radiation; the size of the beam and how it should be aimed; whether to beam the radiation from one direction, or to change directions.

The radiotherapist mentioned before was making drawings and charts to help plan a radiation treatment. The drawings let the physician see exactly how much of the body will receive radiation during the treatment, and how much radiation each part will get.

Then the radiotherapist decides how long each treatment should last, and how long the treatments should continue. The usual time for each treatment is between three and ten minutes. The usual course of treatment lasts from two to ten weeks.

A radiation therapy technician usually gives the actual treatment. Technicians have two years of training beyond high school in the use of radiation for the treatment of disease. There is a shortage of radiation therapy technicians. Very few schools offer training in the field and, in all their work, the technicians are supervised by the radiotherapists.

The technicians first prepare the opening in the head of the machine so it will emit the exact amount of radiation asked for by the radiotherapist. Then the patient is placed in the right position on the table.

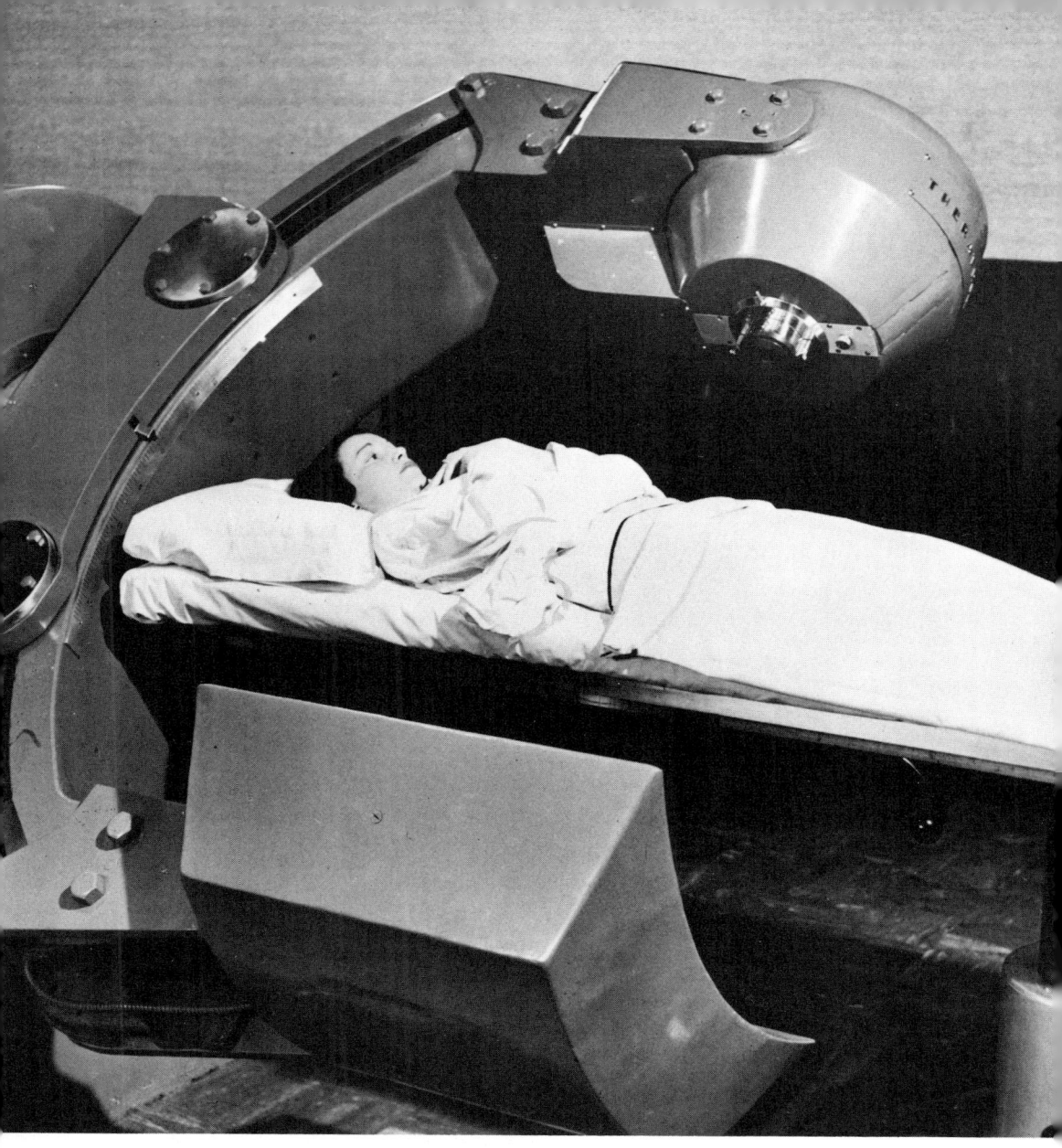

A slug of cobalt-60 in the head of this machine sends out radiation that is similar to X rays.

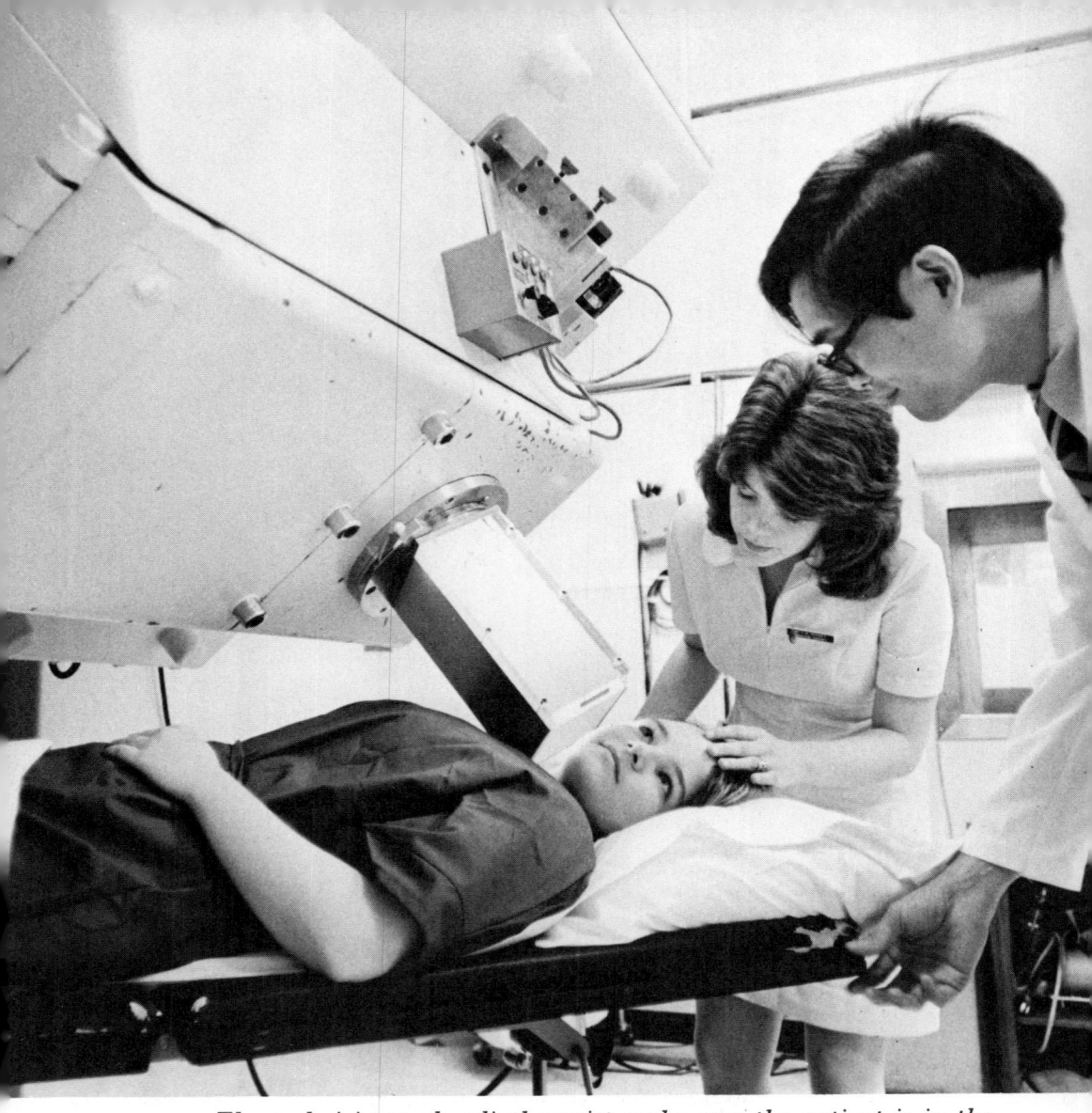

The technician and radiotherapist make sure the patient is in the right position. During the treatment they will watch the patient through the window in the back wall.
PHOTO: MEMORIAL SLOAN-KETTERING CANCER CENTER

This 6½-ton betatron is a super-powerful source of radiation at the Boston University Medical Center. PHOTO: IVAN MASSAR

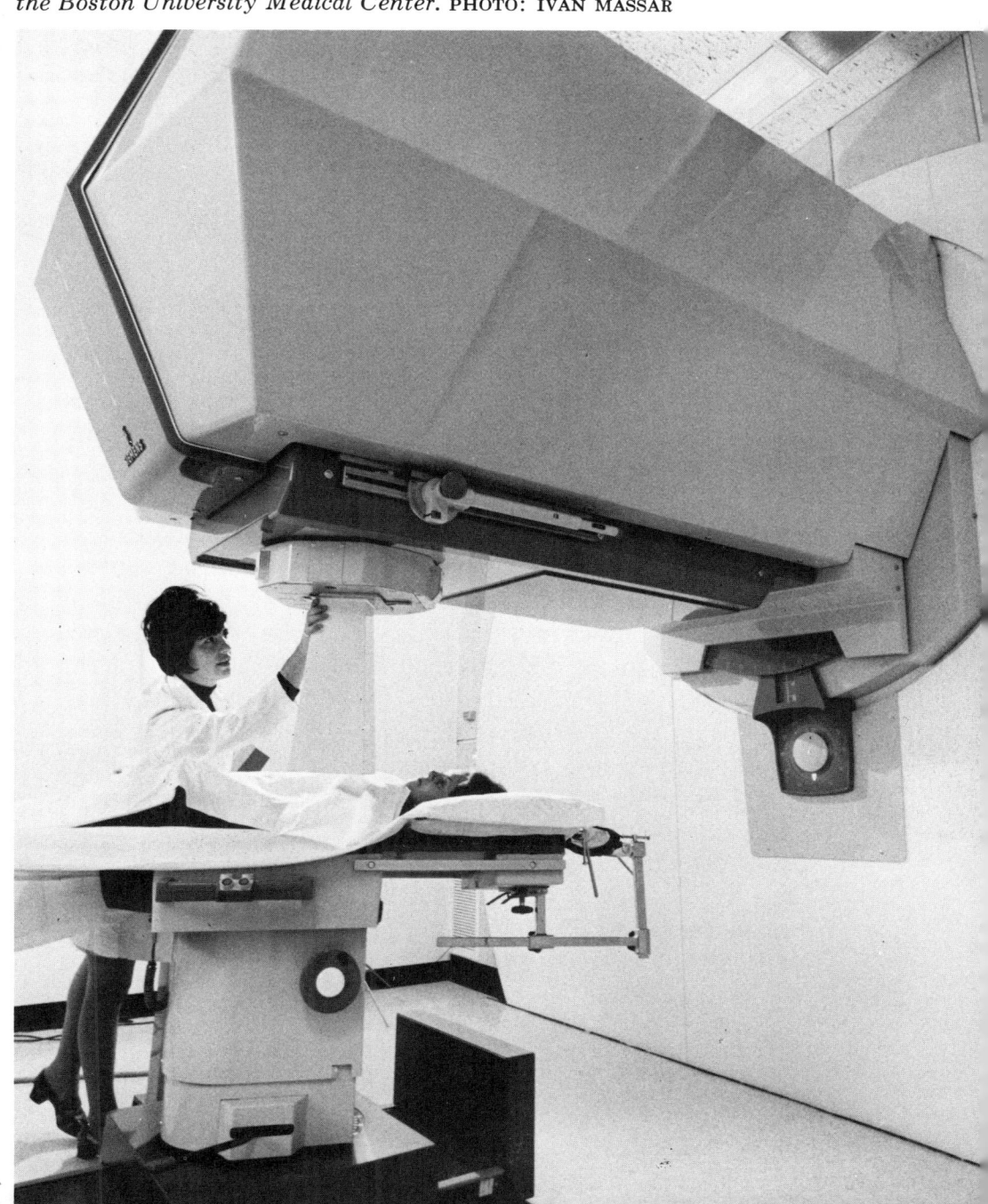

Once the patient and the machine are set, the technician leaves the room. There is a real danger that technicians may be exposed to radiation by accident. So they watch the patients through thick, lead glass windows, or on closed-circuit television.

There are radiotherapists at work on finding different and better sources of radiation. They have had good early results with various kinds of atom smashers, such as the betatron and cyclotron.

In these tools, tiny particles, such as electrons and protons from within the atom, are made to move at fantastically high speeds. They are then aimed at the cancer. In general, the paths of the particles can be controlled better than the paths of the rays. It is believed that particles cause only one-fifth the damage caused to healthy tissue by X rays or gamma rays.

Radiotherapists have also found that radiation kills more cancer cells in the presence of oxygen. Some radiation treatment is now being given in rooms that contain oxygen under high pressure. The results of this treatment are being compared with ordinary radiation treatment. They want to see if the oxygen improves the effect of the radiation.

Most of the time, the radiotherapists beam the radiation at the cancer site from a machine outside the patient's body. Sometimes, though, they find it is better to place the radioactive source right in the cancer growth. They inject tiny needles or grains of radioactive material into the cancer. The radiation that is given off destroys the nearby cancer cells.

You may recall that physicians use small amounts of weak radioisotopes to diagnose some kinds of cancers. Radiotherapists use larger amounts of more powerful radioisotopes to destroy cancer cells. The radioisotopes are attracted to cancer growths. The radiation they give off kills cancer cells.

Radiotherapists plan treatment for patients. They also do research to improve radiation methods and techniques. They perform experiments on different forms of radiation. They study the effects of radiation on cancer cells and normal cells. By treating patients and by doing research, the radiotherapist is helping to make radiation an even more valuable weapon in the fight against cancer.

THE CHEMOTHERAPIST

"I find cancer research one of the most exciting branches of medicine," says Dr. George P. Canellos, Assistant Chief of the Medicine Branch of the National Cancer Institute. "And I feel that I can contribute more in a field where most of the discoveries are yet to be made."

Dr. Canellos is a chemotherapist (pronounced keemotherapist). Just as surgeons operate, and radiotherapists use radiation, chemotherapists use drugs or chemicals to fight cancer.

The idea of using drugs against cancer is only about three decades old. Since then scientists have developed about forty drugs that can be used to control or cure

Dr. George P. Canellos, of the National Cancer Institute, prepares to examine a slide through his microscope.
PHOTO: NATIONAL CANCER INSTITUTE

about ten types of cancers that were invariably fatal ten years ago.

In some cases, the drugs may control the growth of the cancer, causing it to shrink for a while. Frequently this relieves much of the pain of the disease. In other cases, combinations of drugs may permanently eliminate the cancer.

The drugs used by the chemotherapists work in various ways. One group of drugs are cell poisons. They actually kill cells. These drugs kill all types of cells. But the chemotherapists use them because they kill more cancer cells than normal cells.

Another group of drugs interferes with cell growth. They resemble the food that a cell needs for growth. The cells pick up these drugs by mistake. The drugs enter the cells and prevent them from growing and dividing. These drugs also work against both normal and cancer cells. But since some cancer cells divide more rapidly in vital organs, such as the lung or liver, the drugs actually kill more cancer cells than normal cells.

The last group of drugs are hormones. The hormones are chemical substances made in the body. They control the activities and growth of various parts of the body. The chemotherapists use hormones mostly for treating cancer related to the reproductive systems of men and women, as well as some forms of childhood leukemia.

All chemotherapists know that the drugs they use kill healthy cells as well as cancer cells. They are, therefore, very careful in planning the dosage for each patient. They ask themselves: What size dose is best in this case? Should it be given in one big dose, or several small doses? How often should it be repeated?

The chemotherapists also keep a close check on their patients. They watch for any bad side effects that might be caused by the drug treatments. Many of the drugs harm the cells of the stomach lining and bone marrow. These cells are rapidly dividing, and therefore are hurt most by drugs that block cell growth and division.

Dr. Jacqueline Whang, of the Chemotherapy Service at the National Cancer Institute, is spreading cells from a cancer patient on a slide to be studied through a microscope.
PHOTO: NATIONAL INSTITUTES OF HEALTH

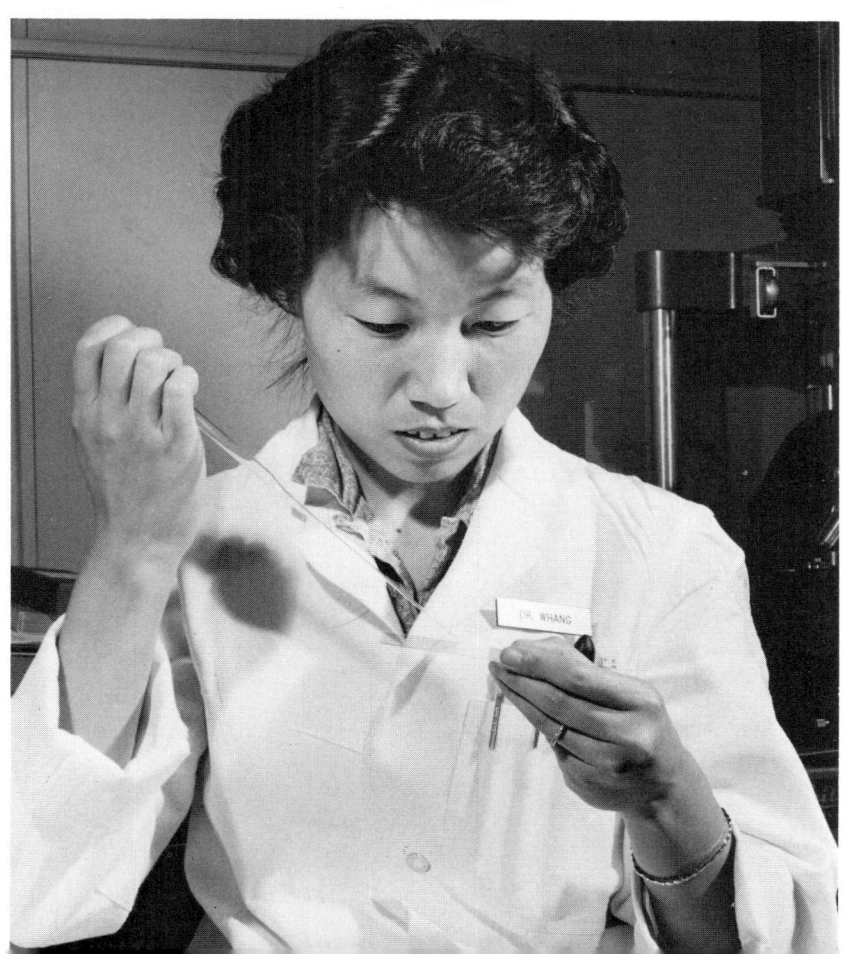

Hormones sometimes cause secondary sex changes in patients who receive this kind of drug. A man might find his voice higher in pitch; a woman might find some hair growing on her face. These are temporary changes, though, and the patient returns to normal when the treatment ends.

Often a cancer drug works well the first time it is given. But if the cancer returns, the drug does not work as well the next time. Chemotherapists are making small changes in the chemistry of some drugs. They hope that they can extend the value of the drugs in this way.

For example, Dr. Vincent T. De Vita, Chief, Medicine Branch, National Cancer Institute, developed a combination of four drugs in 1964, which can cure a substantial percentage of patients with advanced Hodgkin's disease, and prolong the lives of other patients by five to seven years. Survival from advanced Hodgkin's disease used to average no more than two years.

Dr. De Vita's co-worker, Dr. Canellos, and many other researchers, are studying improved combinations of drugs as the most hopeful approach to curing or controlling major cancer killers, such as cancer of the breast and ovary. In the past, most chemotherapists gave their patients only one drug at a time. Now they are finding that they can get much better results by giving four, five or six drugs—all at the same time. Using combinations of drugs and radiotherapy developed by National Cancer Institute physicians, more than 50 percent of the children with a deadly type of leukemia are now surviving free of disease more than five years at certain cancer

Chemotherapists keep a close watch on their patients during treatment. Here a nurse is entering the information on a patient's chart.
PHOTO: NASSAU COUNTY MEDICAL CENTER

centers. Many of these children, who would have died within months, are probably cured.

In 1974, Dr. Canellos reported the results of a study of combination chemotherapy. The subjects were a group of twenty-five patients suffering with advanced breast cancer. All of the patients had been operated on. All had received radiation treatment. Yet the cancer had spread to various other parts of their bodies.

Dr. Canellos knew that about five out of the twenty-five patients should show some improvement, if they were all treated with a single drug. For this experiment, though, Dr. Canellos gave them combination chemotherapy. He used four different drugs at the same time.

The results were most exciting. Seventeen patients showed some improvement. And, in seven cases, all traces of the cancer disappeared for a period of time.

Other experiments in combination chemotherapy show similar results. In a different study of breast cancer, the chemotherapist used a combination of six drugs. About 60 percent of the patients were helped, instead of the 20 percent that are usually helped by a single drug.

Chemotherapists are also exploring ways to combine drug therapy with other methods of treatment, such as surgery and radiation. Combined therapy is a very hopeful new branch of cancer treatment.

Combined therapy increases the chances of destroying cancer cells that have spread. Research studies show that two or three different methods of treatment are more effective than any one method, in many cases.

Cancer treatment today is a team effort. The family physician, the surgeon, the radiotherapist and the chemotherapist work together to plan and carry out the best treatment for the patient. The team approach and combined treatment are now returning more and more cancer patients to healthy, normal lives.

THE IMMUNOLOGIST

Dr. Richard Fisher of the National Cancer Institute is very handy with the Heaf gun. But he does not use this gun to fire bullets. He uses it to save lives.

Dr. Fisher spreads a bit of a special drug on a patient's skin. Then he presses the Heaf gun to the spot and pulls the trigger. Six tiny needles shoot out and break the patient's skin. As they enter the skin, they carry small amounts of the drug with them.

The drug Dr. Fisher uses is not like the drugs used by the chemotherapists. The chemotherapists' drug kills cells. It kills more cancer cells than normal cells, but it kills both. Dr. Fisher's drug helps the patient's own body to

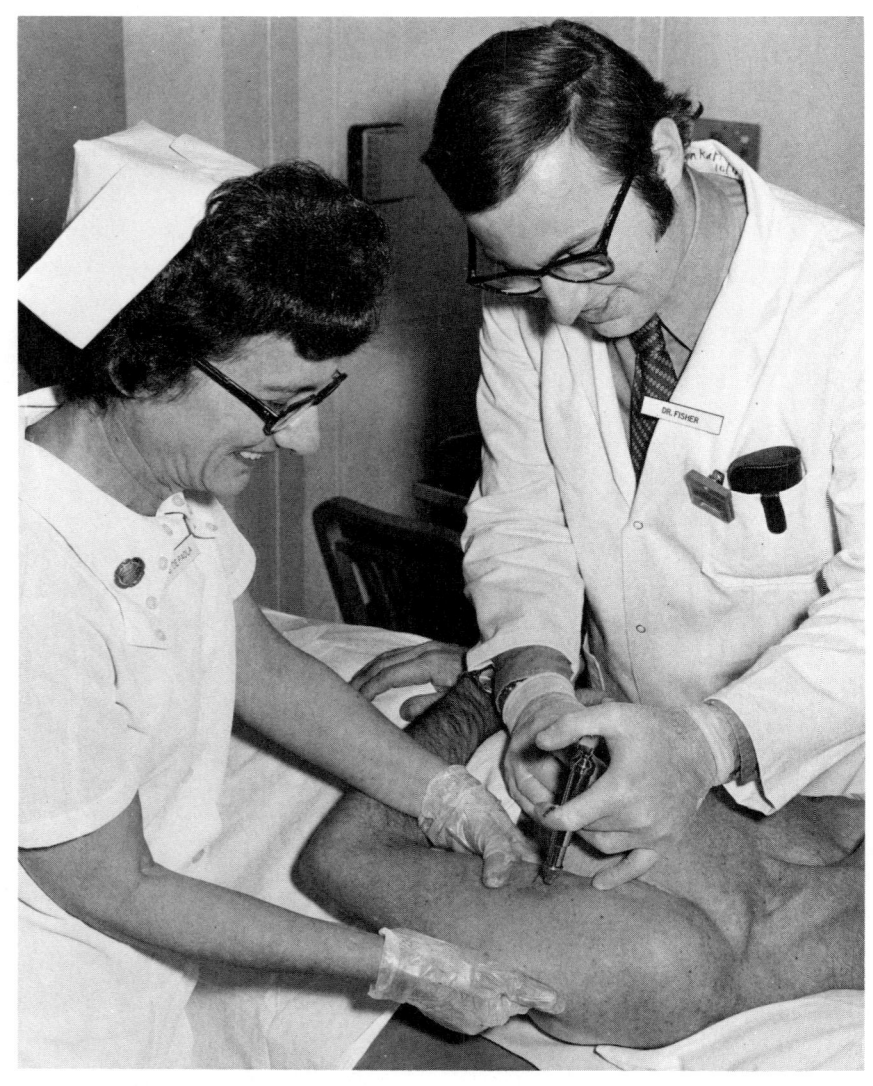

Dr. Richard Fisher uses a Heaf gun to treat a patient.
PHOTO: NATIONAL CANCER INSTITUTE

destroy only cancer cells. It is a way of building up the patient's immune system to fight off the cancer.

The immune system is the body's defense against bacteria and viruses that enter the body and cause disease. It works to destroy anything that enters the body that does not belong there. When the immune system is working well, you are protected against diseases that come from outside causes. When the immune system fails, you become sick.

Cancer scientists are collecting more and more proof of a connection between cancer and the immune system. They point out, for example, that cancer mostly strikes the very old and the very young. These are the two ages when the body's immune system is weakest. As one well-known cancer researcher says, "We've never found a cancer patient in whom something wasn't screwed up immunologically."

The science of immunology dates back nearly 200 years. In 1796, Dr. Edward Jenner injected some pus from a woman's cowpox sore into a healthy boy. The boy became mildly sick with cowpox. The boy's immune system produced antibodies that fought off the cowpox viruses. The antibodies remained in his system.

Then Dr. Jenner injected pus from a smallpox sore into the boy. Smallpox is similar to cowpox, but it is a much more serious and dangerous disease. The antibodies already in the boy's blood were able to destroy the smallpox virus. He did not become sick with smallpox.

Dr. Jenner called this way of protecting against disease vaccination. Different types of vaccines are now used to prevent diseases such as polio, measles, diphtheria and the

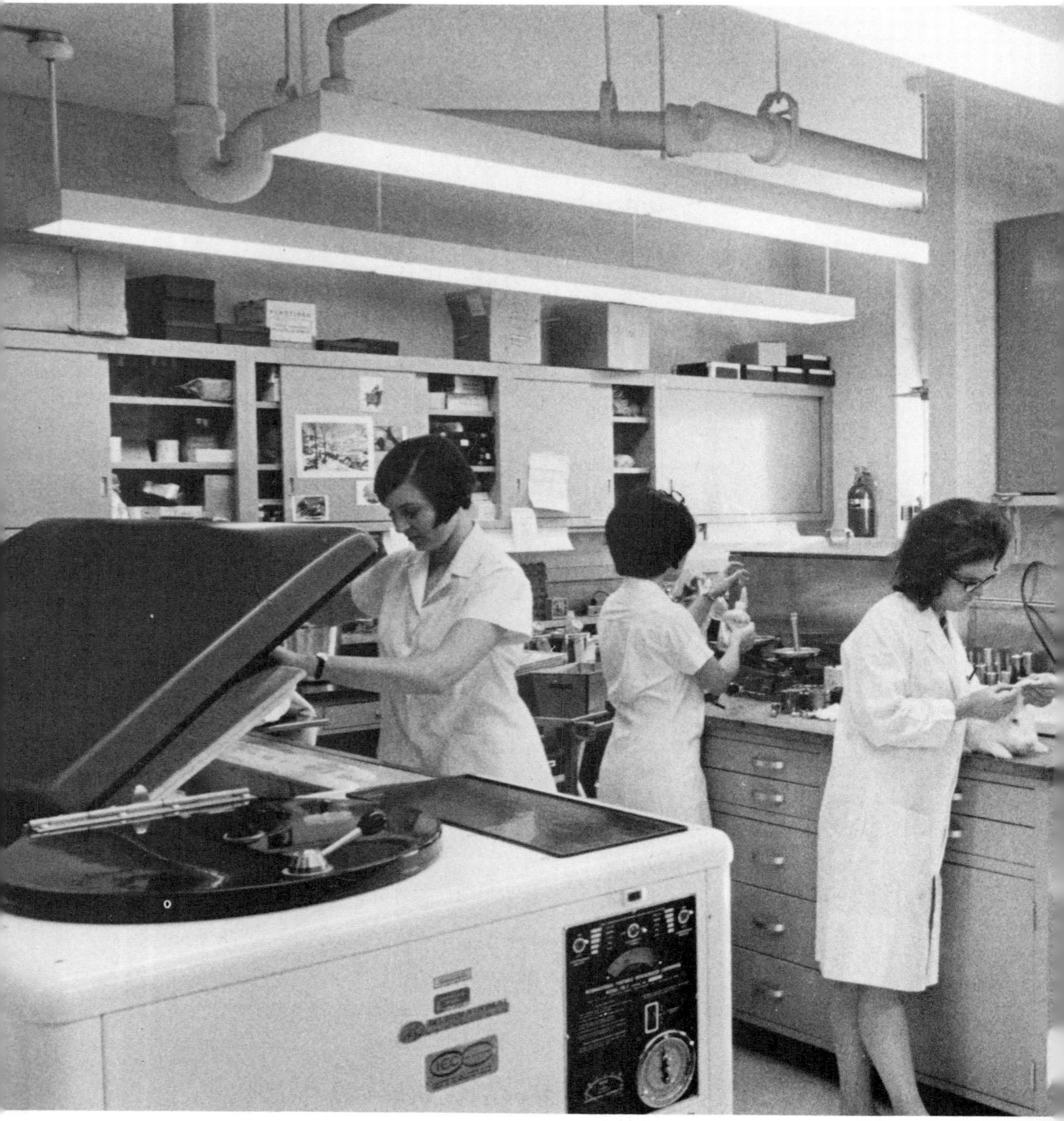

One corner of the Immunology Lab at Memorial Sloan-Kettering Cancer Center. Notice the worker in the center of the picture examining a rabbit's ears.
PHOTO: MEMORIAL SLOAN-KETTERING CANCER CENTER

flu. In these cases, the viruses that cause the disease are treated so that they cannot cause it, or give only a very mild case. Then they are given to the patient. The patient's body produces antibodies to fight the viruses. The antibodies then stay in the body. If the same type of virus later enters the patient's system, the antibodies are there to destroy the viruses. Some cancer researchers are working to develop a vaccine that will, somehow, produce antibodies against cancer.

The drug that Dr. Fisher uses is a vaccine. But it is a vaccine against tuberculosis, a different disease. It is called Bacillus Calmette-Guérin, or BCG. Some years ago Georges Mathé, a French doctor, injected some BCG into several patients in a desperate attempt to control their cancers. He knew BCG turned on the body's immune system to fight the bacteria of tuberculosis. Perhaps, he thought, the immune system would also be able to fight the cancer cells.

The BCG worked. It was not a spectacular success. And other researchers have not been able to duplicate Mathé's findings. But it did extend the life of many of his patients.

Dr. Fisher is part of a team of physicians and laboratory scientists that is running an experiment to learn more about the effect of BCG on human cancers. It is just one of the many experiments, on immunology and cancer, going on at the National Cancer Institute.

The patients for the BCG study are carefully chosen. All of them have received the best possible treatment for their disease, including surgery, radiation and chemotherapy. For one reason or another, these treatments have not stopped the cancer growth.

The scientists explain the goals of this research to the patients. The patients and their families must agree to take part in the experiment, before the scientists will go ahead.

To prepare the vaccine, Dr. Fisher first removes some cells from the patient's cancer. He treats the cells in the lab to weaken them. He adds the weak cells to the BCG. His hope is that, when he injects the mixture of weak cells and BCG, the patient's body will produce antibodies to fight the cancer.

The patients in the study are divided into two groups. The first group is given the BCG and treated cells by means of the Heaf gun or other methods. The second group is given a substance that contains no drugs, but looks the same as the BCG. Neither the physicians nor the patients know who is getting BCG and who is getting the make-believe BCG. Therefore, any changes in the patient's condition must be caused by the drug. It cannot be the result of other factors, such as their faith in BCG.

The researchers carefully watch each patient. How much improvement is there in the group receiving the BCG? Is there any improvement in the group that did not receive the BCG?

An experiment like this one lasts several years. It takes that long to treat enough patients and to see how long those who are "cured" remain healthy. Dr. Fisher and the others are most hopeful. But they must wait before coming to any conclusions.

A most interesting research project, on cancer and the immune system, is going on in a lab of the University of

Twice a week the scientists in the Immunology Branch meet to hear reports on the research the others are doing, and to discuss advances in the field. PHOTO: NATIONAL CANCER INSTITUTE

Washington Medical School in Seattle, Washington. A husband-and-wife team, Drs. Karl and Ingegard Hellstrom, are leading this research.

They have been studying samples of blood taken from patients with different types of cancers and at different stages of the disease. They are comparing these samples with blood from healthy people. The Hellstroms believe that they have found a substance which appears in the blood of patients whose cancer is becoming worse. They found it in 83 percent of the patients whose cancers were growing very fast. They found it in only 16 percent of the patients whose cancer was under control.

The Hellstroms call this substance a blocking factor. It is their belief that the blocking factor blocks the immune system. It does not allow the immune system to attack and kill the cancer cells.

Now that they have found the blocking factor, the Hellstroms are looking for a deblocking factor. They hope that the deblocking factor will free the body's immune system to destroy the cancer.

Karl and Ingegard Hellstrom may have found a deblocking factor. They discovered it in the blood of mice who had recovered from cancer. Early experiments in the test tube make them think that the deblocking factor may get rid of the blocking factor. They are going on to experiment on live lab animals. At the same time, they are trying to find a human deblocking factor.

While doing their research, the Hellstroms stumbled on a very exciting discovery about a type of cancer, called melanoma. Melanoma is a skin cancer that strikes white people about thirty times more often than black people. The Hellstroms found that when blood from a healthy black person is added to melanoma cells from a white person in a test tube, the cancer cells are destroyed.

Could it be that the black person's blood contains a deblocking factor for melanoma? This is a most promising lead. The Hellstroms are hard at work, trying to learn if there really is a deblocking factor, and whether it can be used to fight melanoma in patients.

Much of the research on immunology starts with experiments on mice. PHOTO: NATIONAL INSTITUTES OF HEALTH

The black mouse has a white bandage where a bit of skin was transplanted. The immunologists want to know why some skin transplants are successful, and some are not.
PHOTO: MELVIN BERGER

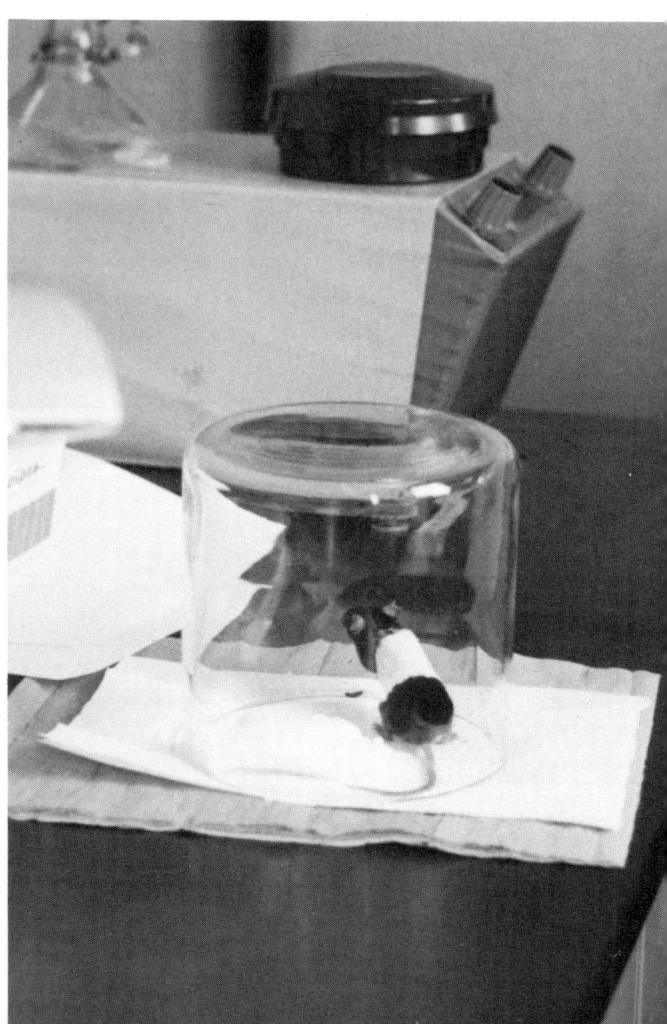

Trying to conquer cancer through the immune system is a very promising line of cancer research. Hundreds of scientists are working in this field.

Their experiments run from using BCG on patients, to transplanting bits of skin from one mouse to another. (Why does the receiving animal's immune system sometimes reject the skin, and sometimes allow it to grow in place?) They run from looking for blocking and deblocking factors, to studying the surface of cancer cells. (Why does the immune system not recognize the invading cancer cell, and attack it?)

Immunology is a bright, new hope for cancer treatment. It could be more successful than surgery which disfigures. And it could be better than radiation and chemotherapy which destroy healthy cells along with the cancer. As one researcher in immunology, Dr. Joseph Robinson, said, "Chemotherapy is like firing a cannon to kill cancer cells. Immunology is getting to the point that it aims a pistol at the cells. And it holds the promise of being able to head straight for the cell, without harming any other part of the body."

CLINICAL LAB WORKERS

It is very early in the morning. The nurse in the cancer hospital goes from room to room. She draws a small sample of blood from each patient, and puts it in a test tube. When all the samples are collected, a nurse's aide places them in a metal rack on a cart. She rolls the cart to the part of the cancer hospital where the labs are located. She stops at a door marked "Clinical Laboratory."

The clinical lab workers will do many different chemical tests on the samples of blood. The results of these tests are very valuable to the physicians who treat the cancer patients.

The test results give the physician vast amounts of information. They tell whether a patient is improving,

The technologist sits at the controls of an autoanalyzer. This machine automatically picks up a few drops of each sample and tests it for chemicals it might contain.
PHOTO: NASSAU COUNTY MEDICAL CENTER

whether a particular treatment is succeeding, how much damage the cancer is doing and so on.

A lab worker brings the cart into the lab. She prepares a work sheet for each sample. It lists the patient's name, hospital number and the various test results needed by the physicians.

At a major cancer center, such as Memorial Sloan-Kettering in New York City, workers in the clinical lab can run 100 different tests on each blood sample. In the course of a year, they perform about one million separate tests. The lab is open twenty-four hours a day, seven days a week.

The lab worker feeds the information on the work sheets into a computer. The computer prepares instructions that tell each worker in the lab exactly which tests to perform.

Most of the workers in a clinical lab are medical technologists. A good number of them are women. Many have college degrees in medical technology. In addition, most of them have received special on-the-job training. After training, the technologists receive a state license that permits them to work in any medical laboratory.

In one of the rooms, a technologist prepares the blood samples for future examination. He pours some of the blood samples into special glass tubes. Then he puts these tubes into a machine called a centrifuge. The centrifuge is like a high-speed merry-go-round. It spins the tubes of blood around at speeds of several thousand revolutions per minute.

In the centrifuge, the two parts of the blood are separated. The solid part, the blood cells, moves to the bottom of the tube. The liquid part, the serum, remains on top. Both parts are then ready for further tests and measurements.

Another technologist loads the serum samples into an autoanalyzer. This machine automatically tests for the chemicals in the blood. It mixes a few drops of the sample with a solution, called a reagent.

If a particular chemical is present, the reagent turns the blood sample a certain color. The color shows that the

67

The physician adds information to the patient's record which is stored in the computer's memory.
PHOTO: NATIONAL INSTITUTES OF HEALTH

chemical is present in the blood. The brightness of the color shows how much of the chemical is present.

An average autoanalyzer can test a blood sample for twelve different chemicals at the same time. And it can test sixty separate samples in an hour. The results go directly to the computer.

Another technologist separates the proteins in a sample of blood serum. Cancer cells produce different proteins from normal cells. The results of this test will tell the physician how widespread the cancer is.

The technologist places a few drops of the serum on a thin strip of plastic. A current of electricity is run through the strip. The electricity pulls the proteins to different points along the plastic. The technologist then removes and stains the strip to bring out the several spots formed by the proteins. She is able to identify each protein by comparing the spots with a printed chart.

The computer occupies one room of the lab. It receives the results of all the tests. It enters the figures on the patient's records. It checks the results. It even signals the technologist if something is wrong, or if the figures seem too high or too low.

The computer prints out a summary of the results for the physician. And finally, it stores the figures in its memory. At any time the physician can review all of a patient's test results.

Every technologist in the clinical lab must be very careful and neat about this work. There is a great need to be accurate and precise. The tests being run are highly important to the physician. They may be a matter of life and death for the patients.

There is also a great need to work quickly. There are

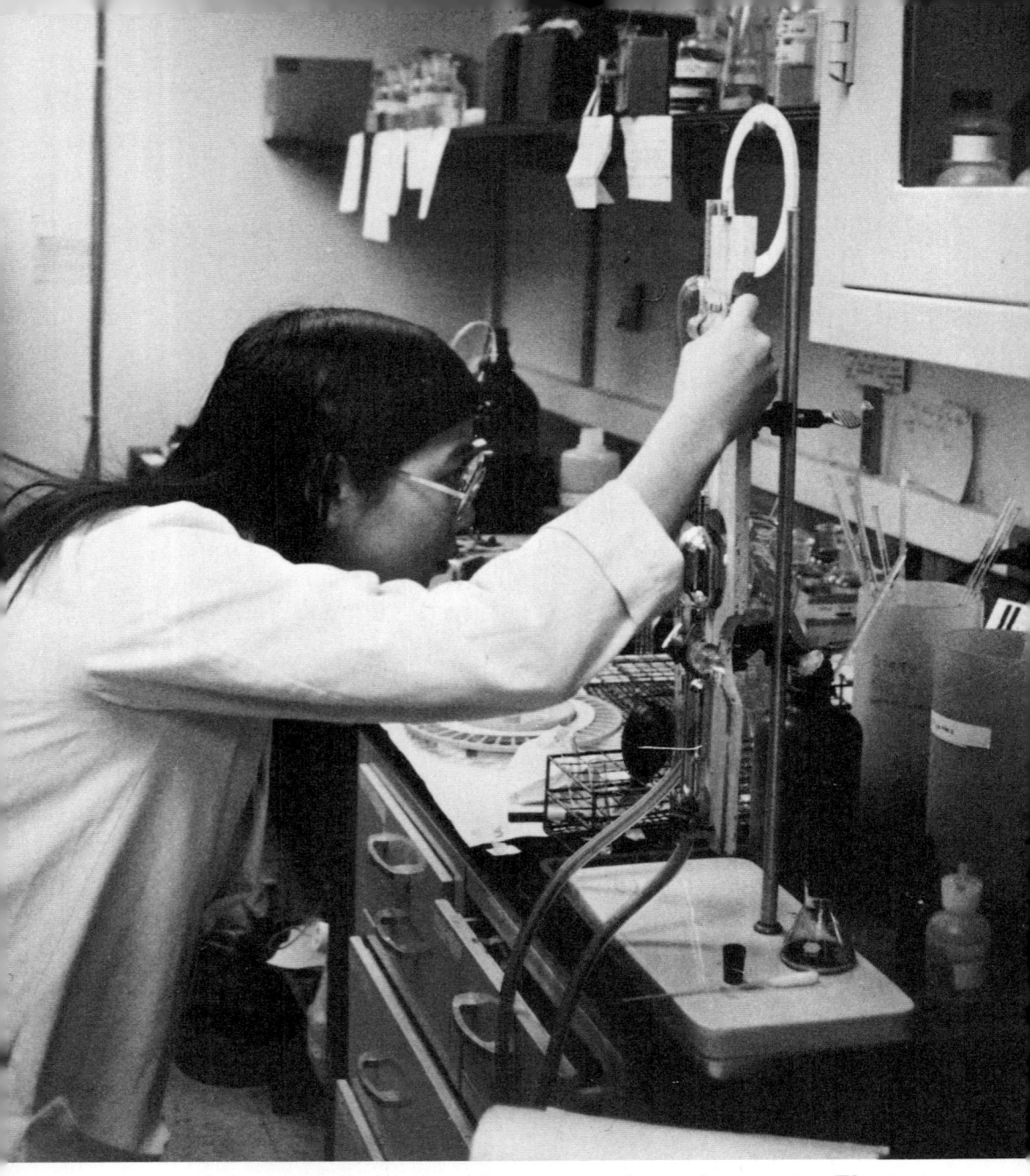

Every technologist must be very precise and accurate. The test results may be a matter of life or death for the patients.
PHOTO: MEMORIAL SLOAN-KETTERING CANCER CENTER

racks of samples, including blood, urine and other body fluids, waiting to be tested. And there are physicians and patients anxiously awaiting the test results.

Even though most technologists do the same tests over and over again, they are seldom bored. The workers are dedicated to their work, and take pride in their accuracy and speed. They are also dedicated to the patients, although they rarely see or meet them. It is possible to follow their cases from the names on the samples and work sheets. They are happy when the test results show that a patient is recovering from cancer.

Biochemists are in charge of most clinical labs. They are ready to help if the technologist runs into a problem.
PHOTO: MEMORIAL SLOAN-KETTERING CANCER CENTER

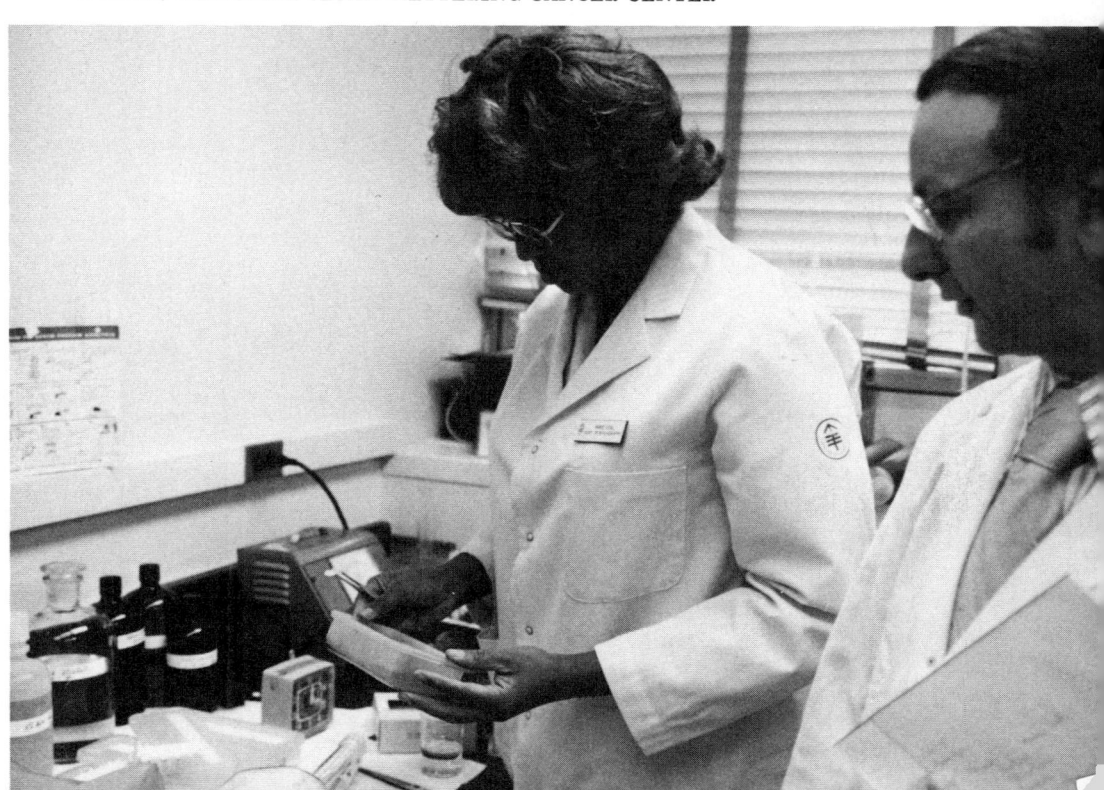

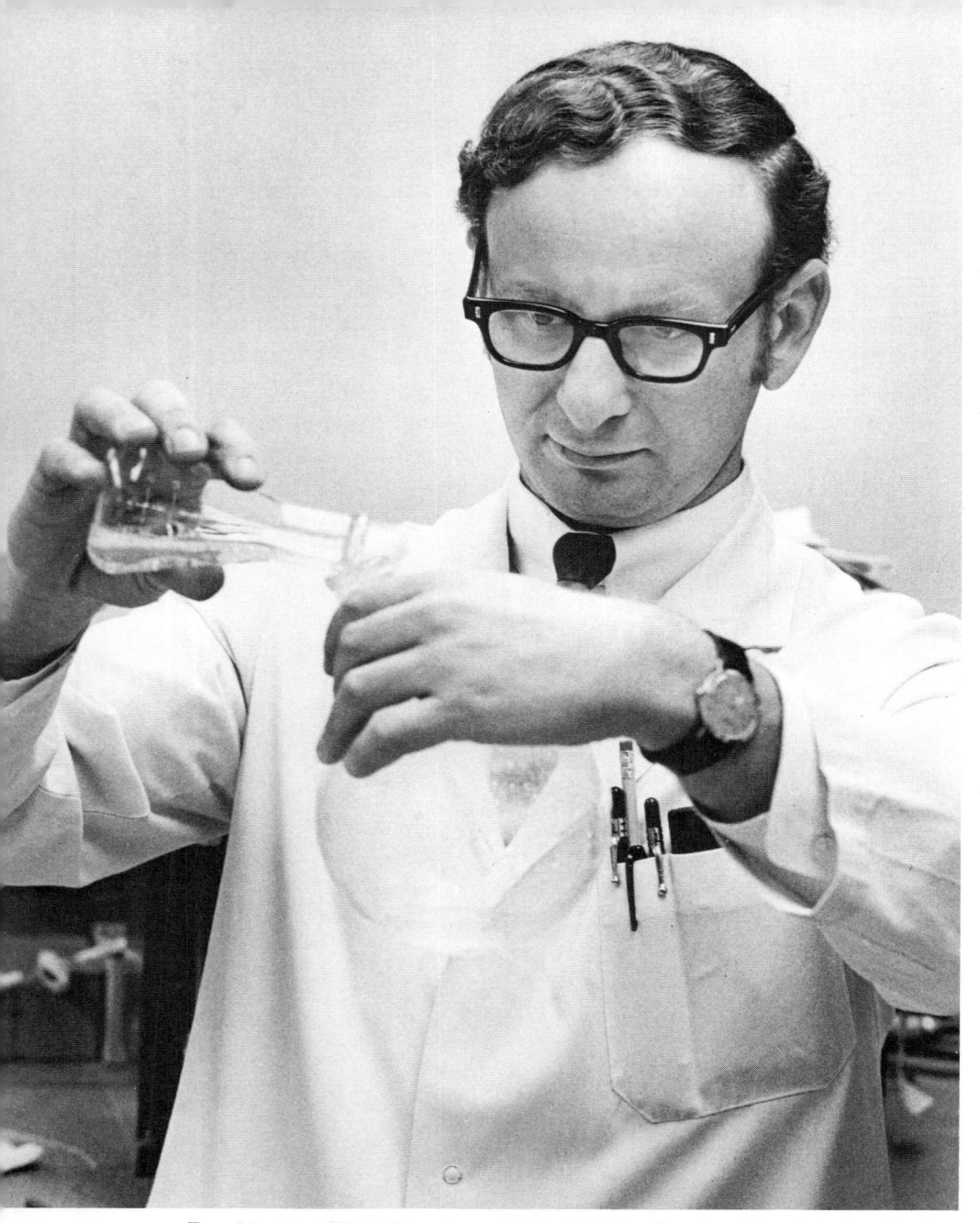

Dr. Martin Fleischer is one of the biochemists in charge of the clinical labs at Memorial Sloan-Kettering Cancer Center.
PHOTO: MEMORIAL SLOAN-KETTERING CANCER CENTER

Scientists direct the clinical labs at cancer centers, such as Sloan-Kettering. They are biochemists, trained in both biology and chemistry. In most cases, they have advanced college degrees. They have a bachelor's degree, for four years of study; a master's degree for another two years; and a doctor of philosophy (Ph.D.) degree for another two or more years.

The biochemists are responsible for the day-to-day running of the lab. They set up the steps for the technologists to follow for each of the tests, and train new workers. They help solve any problems that come up in the lab.

The biochemists run daily checks on the machines to test their accuracy. About one out of every fifty samples sent through the machine is a standard sample. They note the machine's findings. Then they compare the findings with what they know the standard sample contains. If there is any difference, they track down the cause of the error.

These scientists also work closely with the physicians. They may suggest ways that the lab might help provide even better treatment for the patients.

But helping cancer patients and physicians is only part of the work of the clinical lab. Workers here are also involved in original research. Most of the experiments are on the chemistry and biology of the blood.

In a few long-range experiments, researchers are looking for chemicals in the blood of cancer victims. Perhaps this will lead to a blood test for the early detection and diagnosis of cancer. Other experimenters are seeking ways to use the results of the lab tests to tell even more about where the cancer is located and its size.

Dr. Martin Fleischer is one of the biochemists in charge of the clinical lab at Memorial Sloan-Kettering. He is proud of the role the clinical lab workers play in caring for cancer patients. And he is hopeful that researchers in the lab will discover new methods and tools to improve medical care for cancer patients.

THE PATHOLOGIST

A man sat hunched over the microscope. All of his attention was focused on the slide he was examining. He had to decide if the cells on the slide were normal or cancer cells. He carefully studied every feature of the cells. He wanted to be positive that his findings were correct.

The man at the microscope was a pathologist. Pathologists are medical doctors. They study the tissues and organs of the body, looking for changes caused by disease.

The tissue that the pathologist was examining was taken from a patient in a biopsy. A surgeon had snipped out some tissue from a growth. The operating room nurse

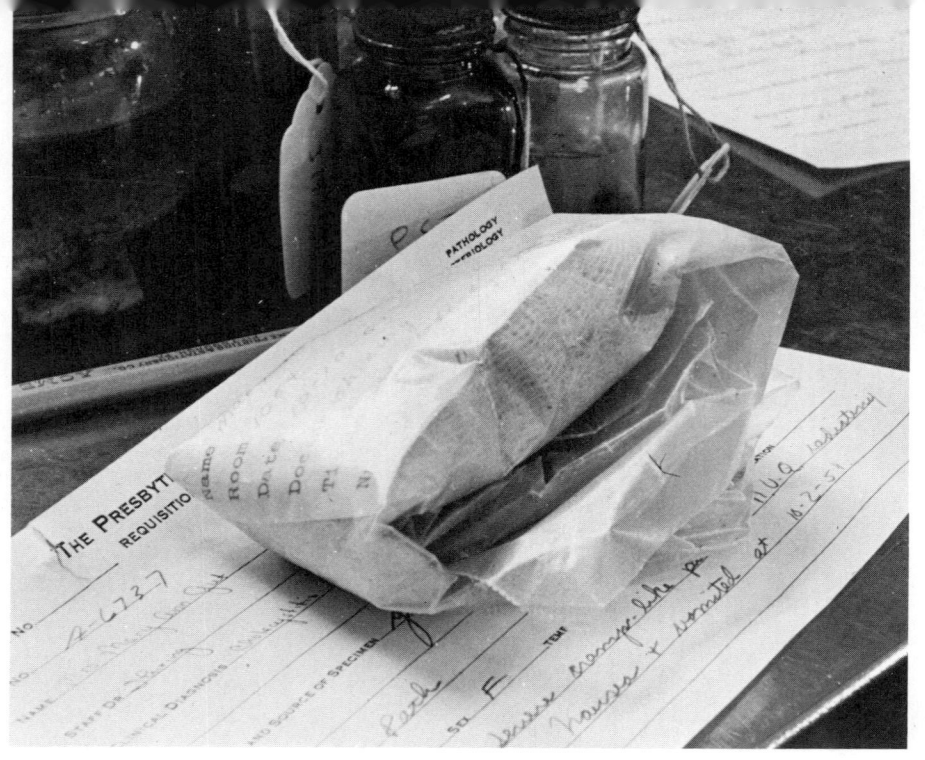

The specimen arrives at the pathology lab, ready to be examined by the pathologist. PHOTO: HAROLD CORSINI

spoke on the telephone to the pathology lab several floors below.

"This is O.R. 3," she said. "We're sending a biopsy specimen down. We'll be waiting for your report."

Within minutes the specimen arrived through a tube that runs from the operating room to the pathology lab. The pathologist took it from its container and brought it to a lab bench. He placed it on a paper towel on the bench. He looked it over closely. The tissue was about the size of a peanut.

He wanted to study the individual cells under a microscope. Using a surgeon's knife, he cut out a small section of the specimen which looked as though it might contain cancer cells. He placed the section in a small metal basket.

The technologist, who was standing by, took the basket. Her job was to prepare a microscope slide. For microscope study, the tissue must be cut into thin slices, called sections. The sections must be thin enough for light to pass through.

But the tissue was too soft to be sliced. It had to be made solid. The fastest way to make tissue solid is to freeze it.

The technologist placed a small amount of a chemical compound on the sample. She plunged it into a tube of liquid nitrogen. Within moments, the specimen was frozen into a solid block.

She placed the frozen specimen in a special refrigerated cabinet. Inside the cabinet is a device called a microtome. It is used to cut sections from the specimen. Quickly and expertly the worker cut a section, and placed it on a glass slide.

It is almost impossible to see a very thin tissue section on a slide. To make it visible, the technologist must stain it. She dipped the slide into different solutions. Presently the section was stained bright pink and purple.

A technician quickly brought the stained slide over to the pathologist. He placed the slide on the stage of his microscope. He began to search for any sign of cancer cells.

After a while, the pathologist looked up from the microscope. He reached for the nearby telephone.

"O.R. 3, please," he asked. "This is pathology. We've

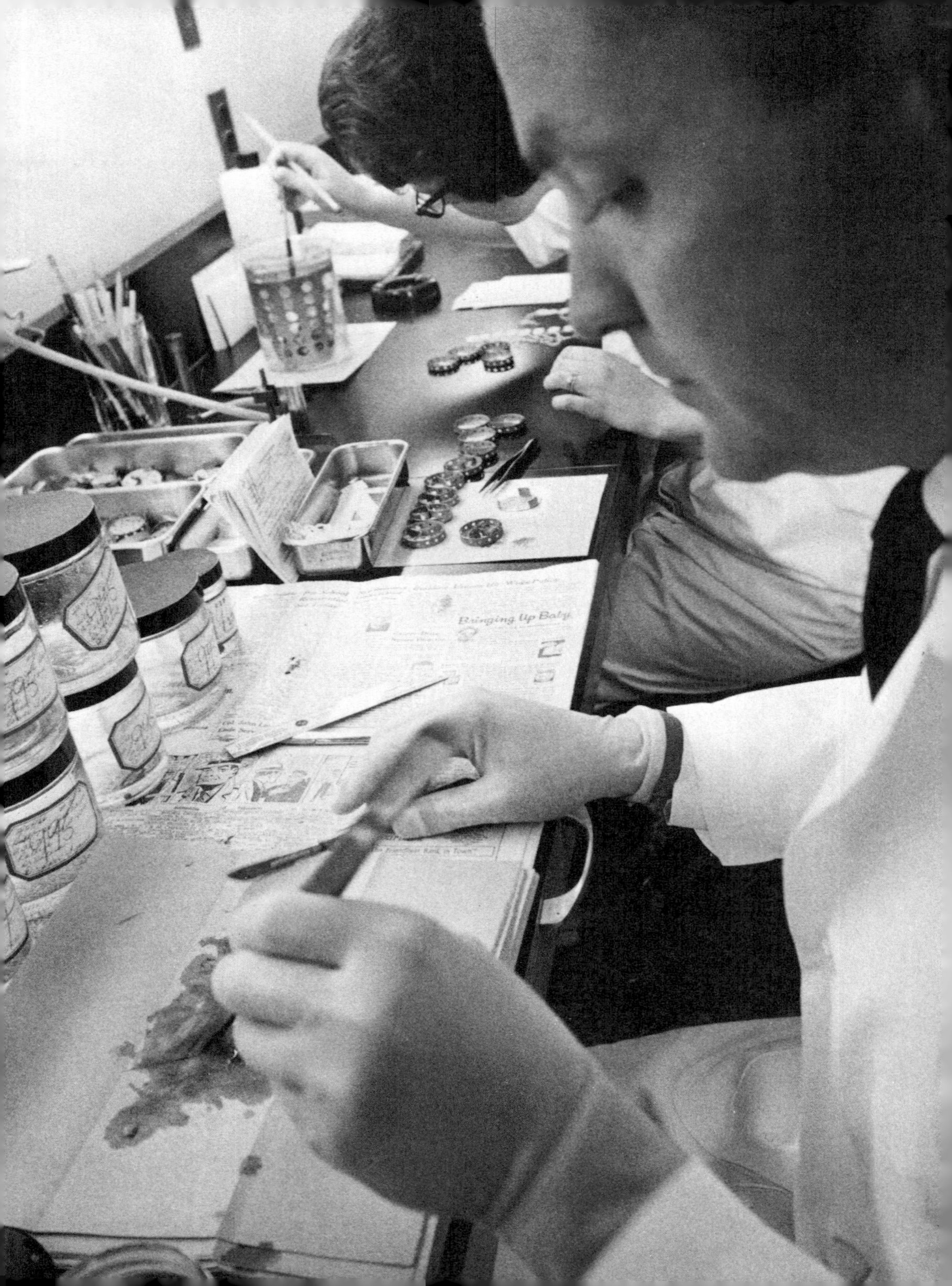
Bringing Up Baby

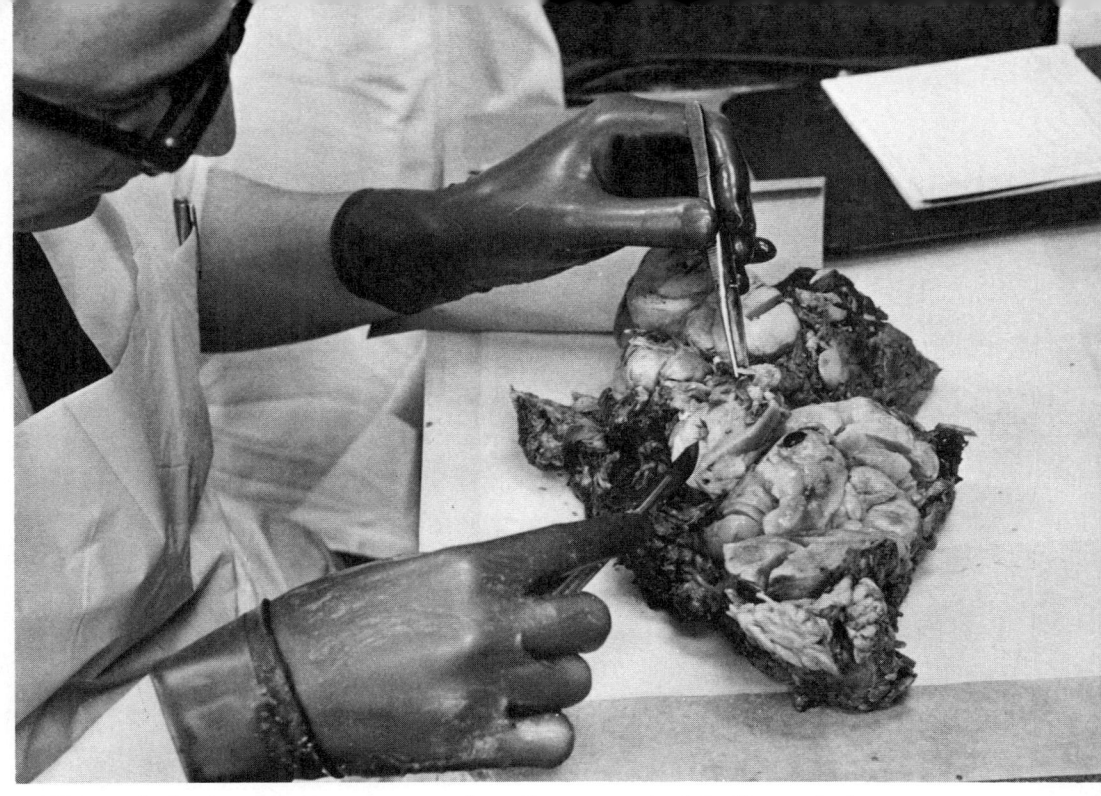

The pathologist uses tweezers and a sharp surgical knife to help him do a gross examination of a cancer growth removed by the surgeon. PHOTO: MEMORIAL SLOAN-KETTERING CANCER CENTER

got good news. The specimen is benign. No sign of cancer."

The clock on the wall showed that only five minutes had passed since the tissue arrived from the operating room. Since it was not a cancer, the surgeon stitched up the small cut of the biopsy and sent the patient back to his hospital room to recover.

The pathology lab in a busy cancer center gets many calls each day for quick biopsy reports. The pathologist handles these calls promptly.

The pathologist looks over the tissue. He will place the parts that need further study into the metal baskets near the technologist.
PHOTO: ARTHUR LEIPZIG

But most pathology reports are not needed in such a hurry. They are reports on tissue from patients known to have cancer. The pathologist examines the specimens to learn more about the disease. This information helps the physicians plan future treatment. It also acts as a double check, to make sure that the original diagnosis was correct.

In these cases, the specimen is brought to a desk at the entrance to the pathology lab. A technician prepares a lab form that stays with the specimen. The form lists the patient's and physician's names. It gives the specimen a lab number. Also included is a sketch that shows which part of the body the specimen came from; comments by the physician on what disease he suspects; and other information helpful to the pathologist making the examination.

When the pathologist receives the tissue and form, an overall study is done first. This is called a "gross." Sometimes the pathologist cuts the specimen open to see more. What is the size, shape, color and condition of the specimen? Is there any feature that is striking or unusual? What is the evidence of disease?

The pathologist often reports the observations of the gross examination into a microphone over the lab bench. The microphone is connected to a tape recorder. Later, the pathologist's comments are typed onto the patient's records.

Next, the pathologist cuts out any parts of the specimen that should be looked at more closely under a microscope. These parts are placed into small metal baskets.

Freezing is only a quick, temporary method of making a specimen stiff enough to slice. The usual, and more accurate, way is to embed the tissue in paraffin, a material similar to candle wax.

A technician places the basket containing the tissue in a special machine, called an autotechnicon. The autotechnicon automatically dips the specimen into various solutions that preserve the tissue and embed it in paraffin.

The specimens are placed in the autotechnicon during the day. The machines are turned on at night. The next morning, the tissue is set in a solid block of paraffin.

The technologist removes the tissue sample set in a block of paraffin. The autotechnicon automatically dipped it into the various solutions to preserve and embed the tissue.
PHOTO: ARTHUR LEIPZIG

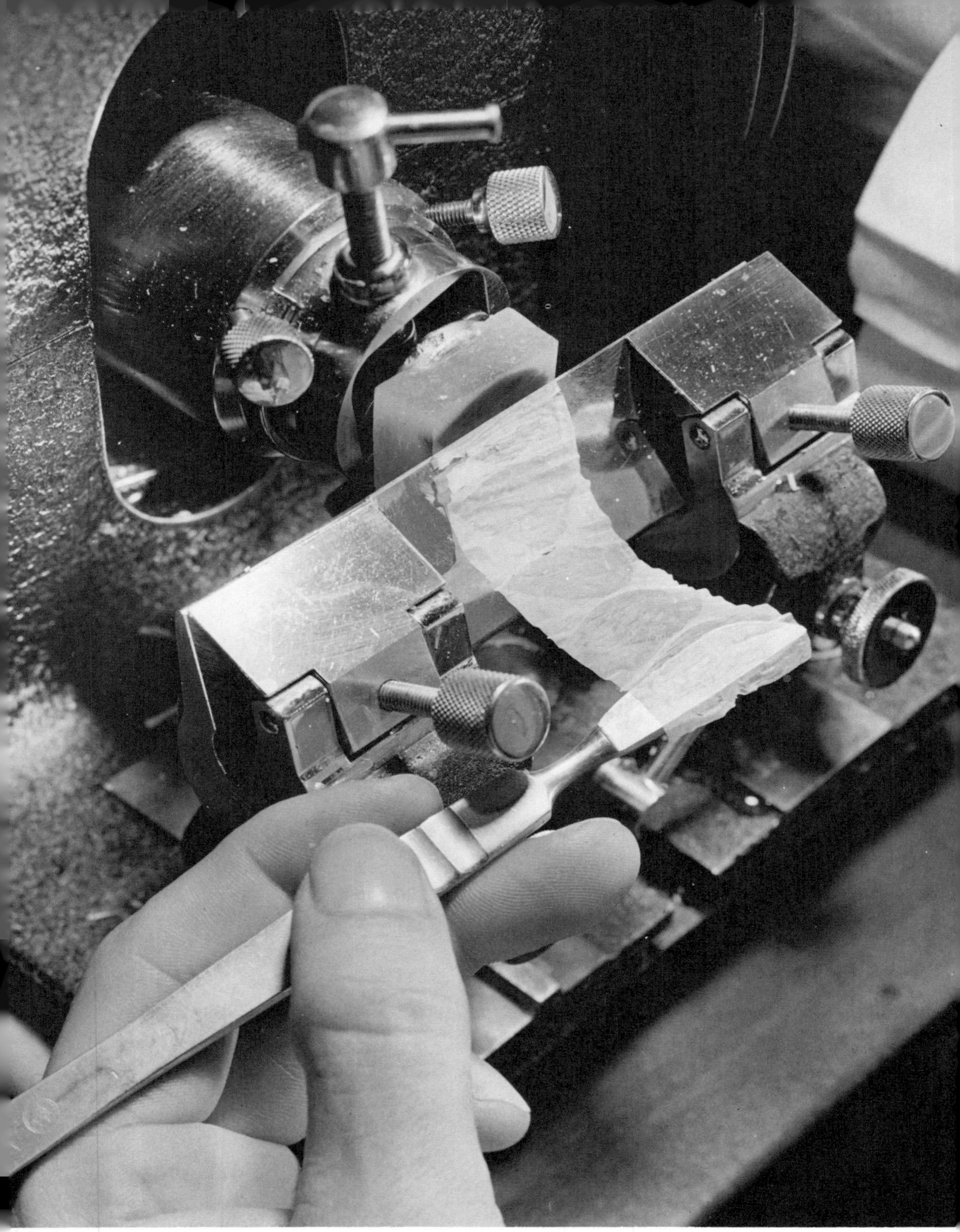

A technologist uses the microtome to cut the sections needed for microscopic study. By turning the large wheel on the side of the microtome, the technologist moves a knife blade back and forth, and quickly makes about twenty slices.

Moving more slowly and carefully, she gets one slice that will give the pathologist the best idea of the entire specimen, places this section on a clean glass slide. On the side of the slide she writes the patient's lab number.

Another technologist places the slide in a small lab oven to melt the paraffin, leaving just the tissue section on the slide. He dips it in and out of a long row of solutions to stain it. Then he places a cover slip—a thin piece of glass—over the section. The slide is ready to be looked at by the pathologist.

It takes about twenty-four hours for the physician to get a routine pathology report. A copy of the report, the slide and the findings of the gross examination are placed in the patient's file. They are useful in planning future treatments. They are also necessary for any research projects that study the effect of disease on the body.

The technologists who work in the pathology lab are high school graduates. Many have college degrees. They also receive special training in the pathology lab in which they work, and become experts in one of the operations of the pathology lab.

The helpers in the lab are the technicians. There are no educational requirements for this position. They are trained in the lab. All they need is to be able to read and write well, a willingness to learn, and neat, careful work habits.

A close-up of a microtome with the paraffin block in the center. The knife goes up and down in front of it. The gray shapes in the paraffin ribbon are the tissue sections. The technologist will choose the best one to be made into a slide.
PHOTO: NATIONAL INSTITUTES OF HEALTH

All the workers in the pathology lab—from the technician to the highly trained pathologists—are dedicated to helping the cancer patient. They produce reports accurately and speedily. They search for ways to improve the services they offer. And they do original research in cancer disease.

Many of the advances in treating and understanding cancer are due to the skill and knowledge of the pathologists and others who work with them.

CANCER-CAUSE RESEARCHERS

The technician walks into the animal room and pulls out one of the drawerlike cages, in which the laboratory mice are kept. He reaches in and lifts up one of the white mice.

Holding it lightly in his left hand, he examines the mouse's belly. Then he dips a fine paintbrush into a small jar of dark-brown liquid, and brushes a little of the liquid on the mouse's belly. He drops the animal back into its cage and pulls out the next cage.

He repeats the examination and treatment on twenty of the many mice in the room, and makes notes on each mouse that he handles.

This technician is part of a research project studying

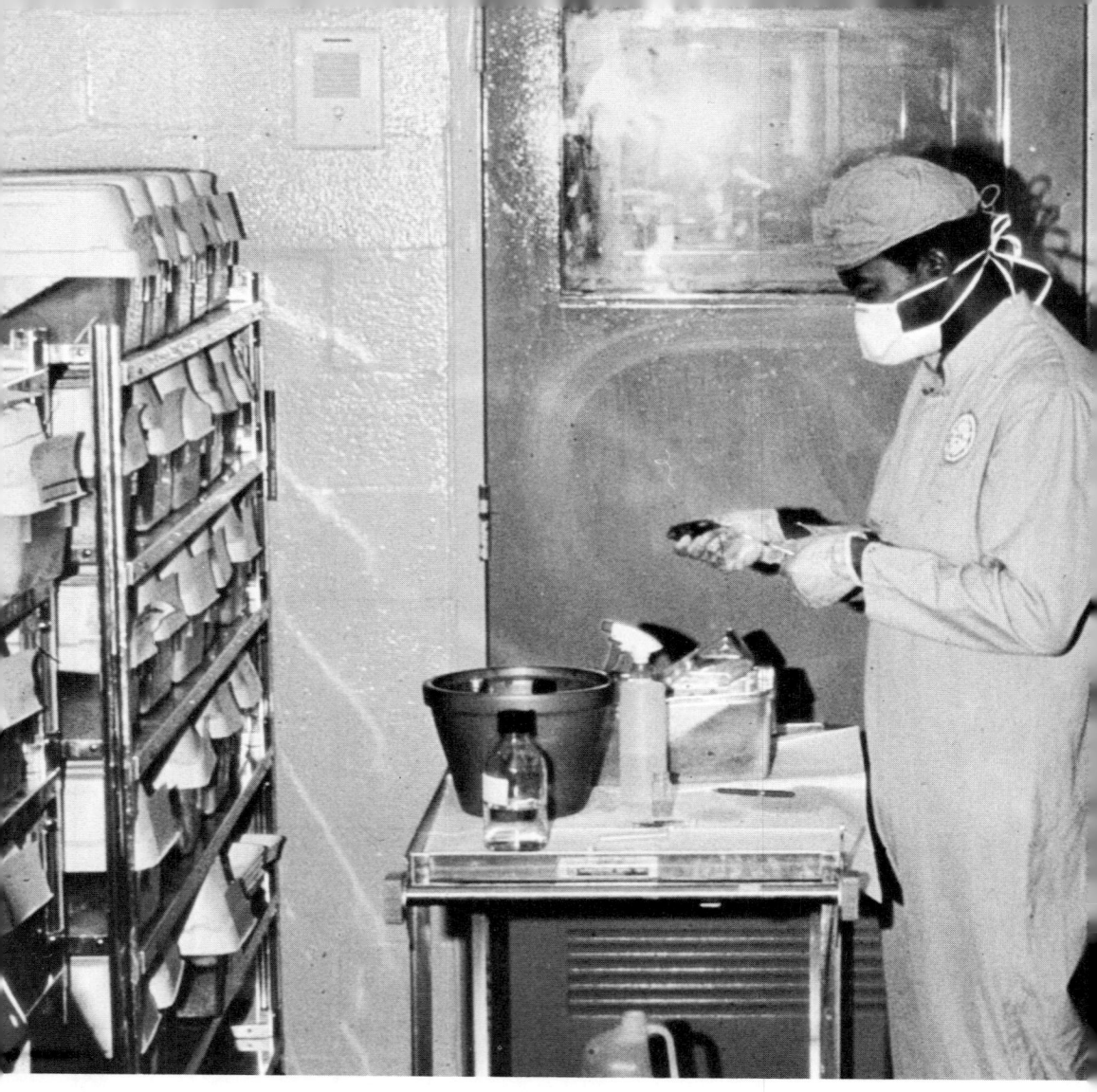

The technician wears gloves, a mask and a cap to protect him as he applies chemicals that might cause cancer to lab mice.
PHOTO: NATIONAL CANCER INSTITUTE

why a high percentage of workers in a certain plastics factory are developing cancer of the liver. Scientists suspect that the cancer is caused by one of the chemicals handled by the workers.

The scientists cannot experiment on humans with substances that may cause cancer. They planned this experiment to observe the effect of the chemical on laboratory mice. The information they get from this animal research will tell them more about the effect of this chemical on humans.

Most researchers on the causes of cancer use mice for their experiments. Mice are cheap and are easy to raise. They have a short life cycle, so they show the results of the experiment very quickly. And finally, cancer in mice is similar to cancer in people. The scientists are able to transfer findings in experiments with mice to human beings.

The researchers take very good care of their lab animals. They feed them well, keep them clean and comfortable and never mistreat them. If an animal might feel pain in an experiment, it is given an anesthetic so it feels nothing.

Experimental mice are bred within their own family. They are all very much alike in most ways. Pure strains of mice react the same way in the various experiments.

Researchers who test cancer-causing chemicals try to give the mice the chemical in the same way that it usually enters the human body. Chemicals that people touch are painted on the skin of lab mice. In other cases, the researchers feed it, inject it or have the animal breathe the substance.

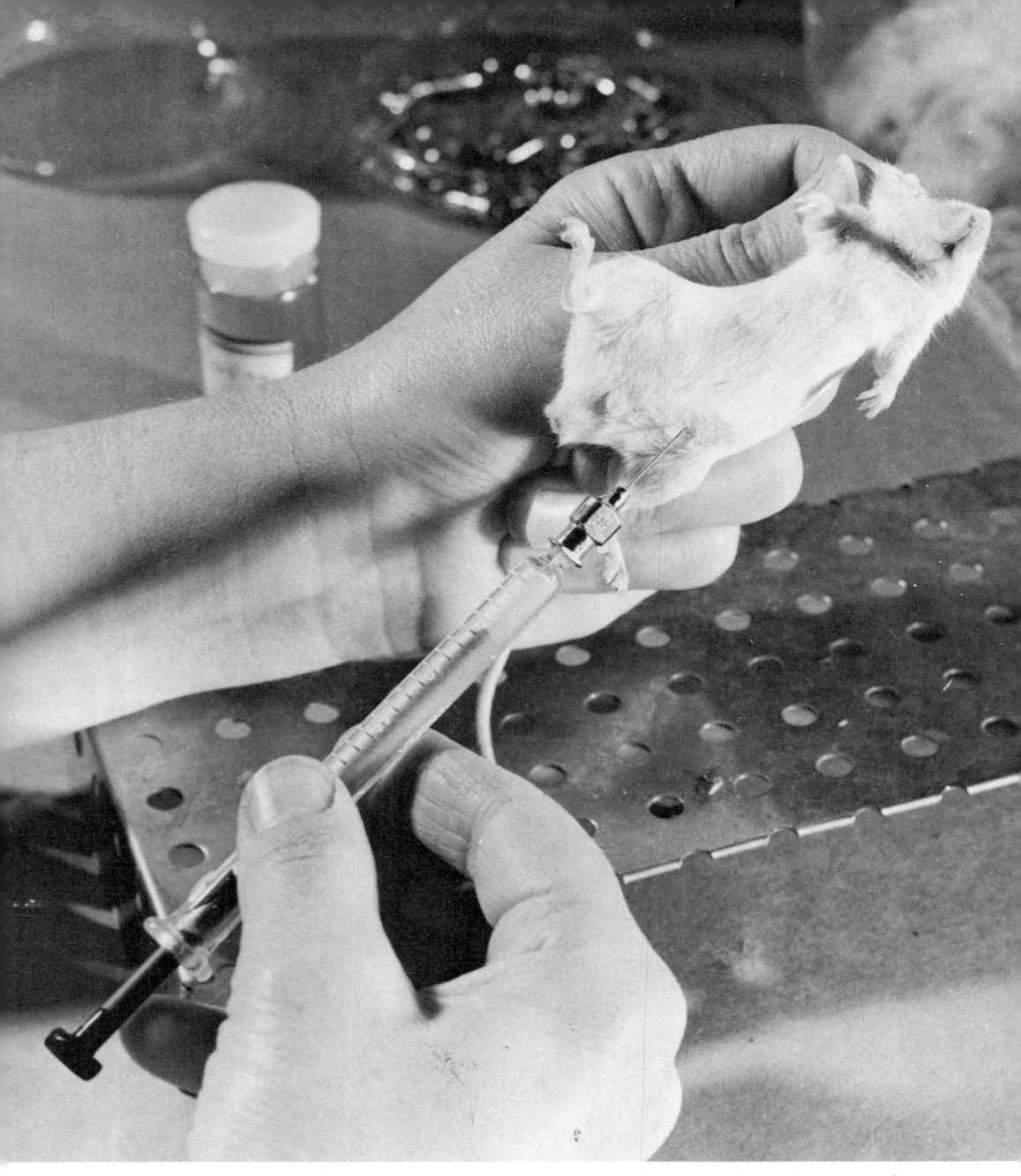

Researchers often test cancer-causing chemicals by injecting the substances into the bodies of laboratory mice.
PHOTO: NATIONAL INSTITUTES OF HEALTH

The scientists often divide the mice into two groups. The mice in the first group are given the chemical in some way. The mice in the second group are not exposed to the chemical.

The scientists then compare the mice. If a cancer develops, it usually appears in about three months. If a cancer does not appear within two years, most researchers rule out that chemical as a cause of cancer.

Over 1,000 chemicals that cause cancer in animals have already been found. Included in this list are many plastic and dye compounds made from oil or coal; certain metals, such as nickel, chromium and cadmium; some minerals, such as asbestos; chemicals used to kill weeds and to fatten animals; smoke from burning cigarettes and badly polluted air.

Once the researchers find a chemical that causes cancer in mice, they still have several questions to answer: How powerful a cause of cancer is this chemical? The scientists have learned that the sooner the cancer appears, and the more widespread it is in the animal's body, the more powerful the cause.

How does the chemical cause the cancer? Researchers try to follow the route and action of the chemical inside the animal's body. They study the organs and tissues to see the exact changes brought about by the chemical.

Does it also cause cancer in larger animals? Chemicals found to cause cancer in mice are also tested on other research animals, such as rabbits, guinea pigs, cats, dogs and monkeys. The results of these tests tell the scientists even more about the possibility that this chemical causes cancer in humans.

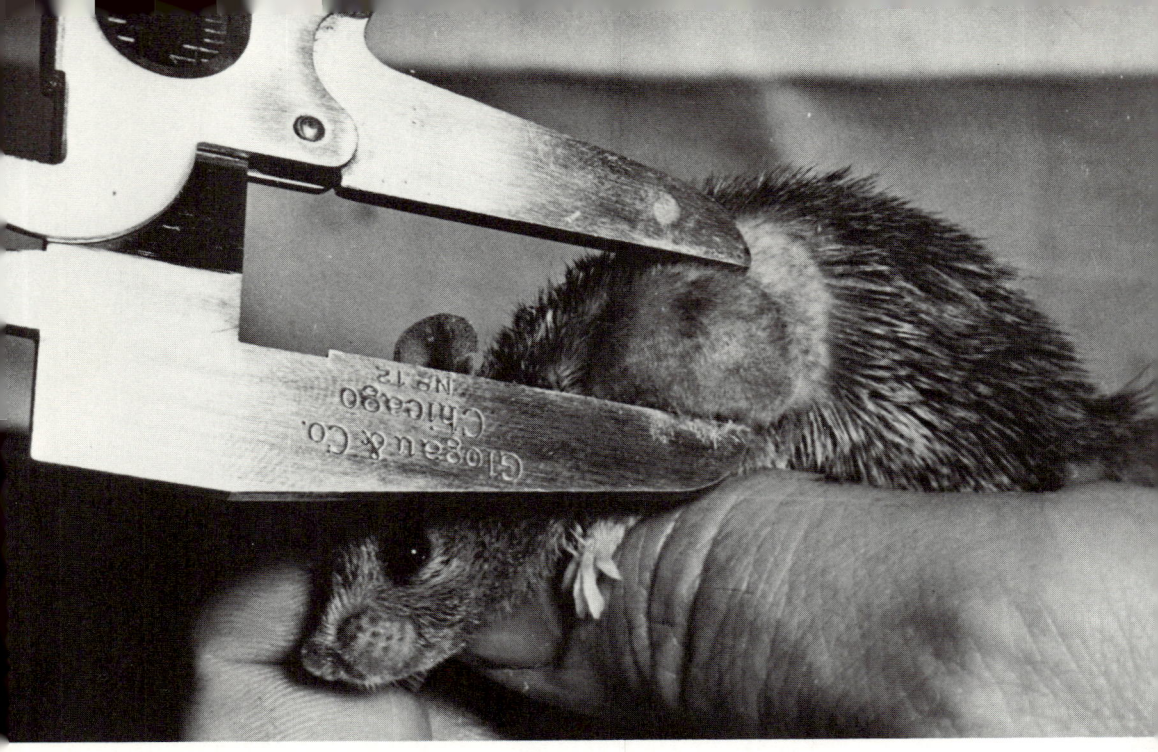

The scientist measures the exact size of a tumor in an experimental mouse. PHOTO: NATIONAL INSTITUTES OF HEALTH

Not all scientists who study the causes of cancer, however, work in labs. Other cancer-cause researchers work in offices with pencil and paper, charts and graphs, and computers.

These scientists, called statisticians, study the facts and figures on the spread of cancer. They collect information on the numbers of people struck with cancer and the types of cancer. Then they try to find out more about cancer patients—age, sex, occupation, diet, smoking habits, general health, city or farm environment, history of cancer in family and other information that may give a clue to the cause of cancer.

The research on the chemicals used in the plastics factory was begun by a statistician. He noticed that the cancer rate among the factory workers was higher than the normal rate. He suggested that the lab scientists try to find a chemical cause of cancer among those used in the factory.

Statisticians are working closely with the lab scientists in researching smoking as a cause of lung cancer. Part of the statistical research is "backward research." Scientists read the reports of state health departments. How many people developed lung cancer last year? How many of the victims smoked cigarettes? How much did they smoke? How long had they been smoking?

Part of the research is "forward research." The National Cancer Institute and the American Cancer Society are following the health of nearly a half-million people. They keep figures on how much each one smokes. They will be informed of all cases of lung cancer that develop.

The statisticians are finding, both in their backward and forward studies, that the chances of developing cancer are up to twenty times greater for smokers than for nonsmokers.

Meanwhile other scientists are testing cigarette smoke on lab animals. They are exposing them to cigarette smoke. They find that the animals develop cancers just as humans do.

In one study, lab scientists paint various chemicals found in cigarette smoke on mice. They have already found twelve separate chemicals in cigarette smoke that cause cancer in mice. The results of these experiments

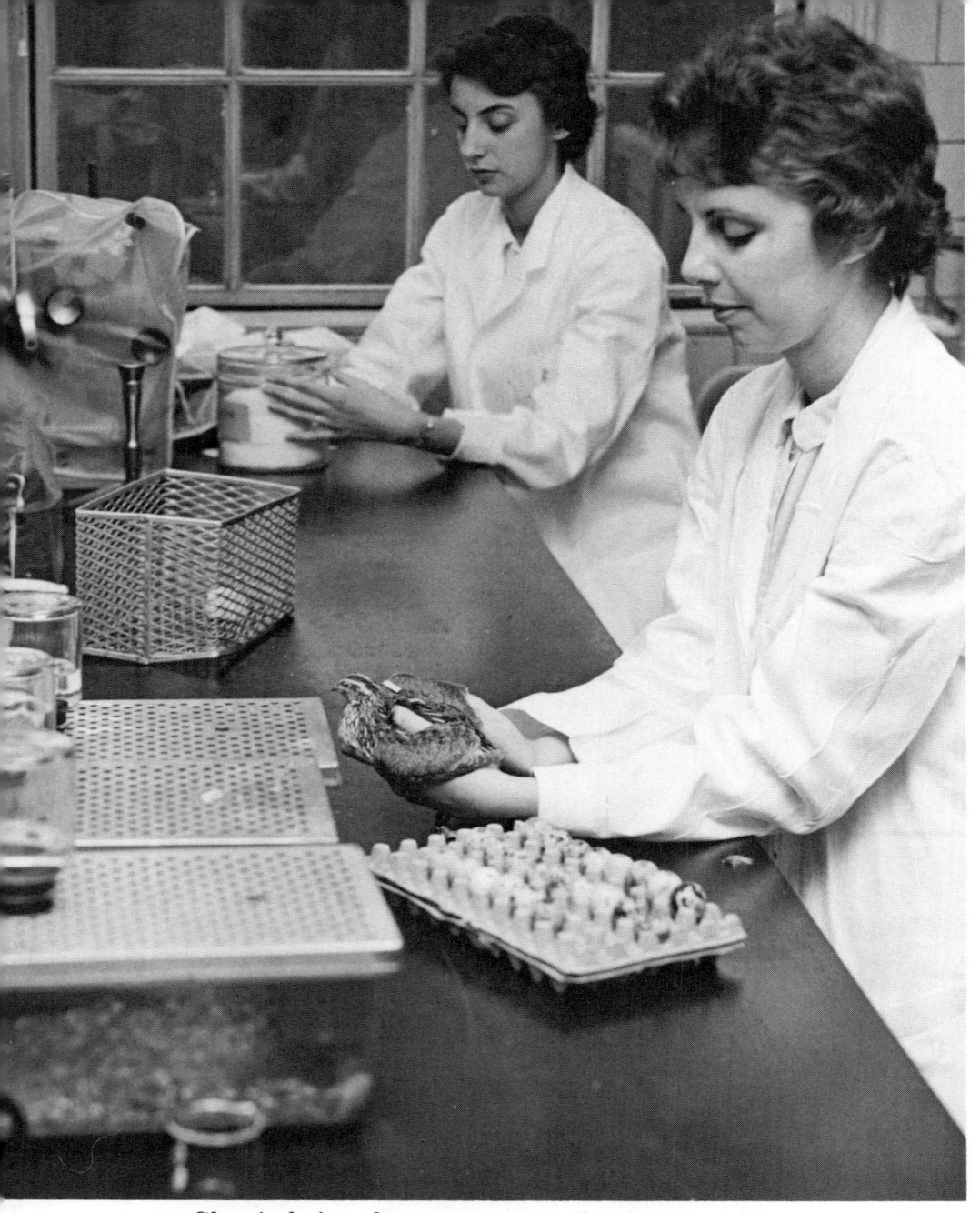

Chemicals found to cause cancer in laboratory mice are tested on other animals such as this Japanese quail.
PHOTO: NATIONAL INSTITUTES OF HEALTH

This scientist is caring for newborn twin monkeys. They will be injected with cells from human cancer patients to learn more about the cause of human cancers.
PHOTO: NATIONAL INSTITUTES OF HEALTH

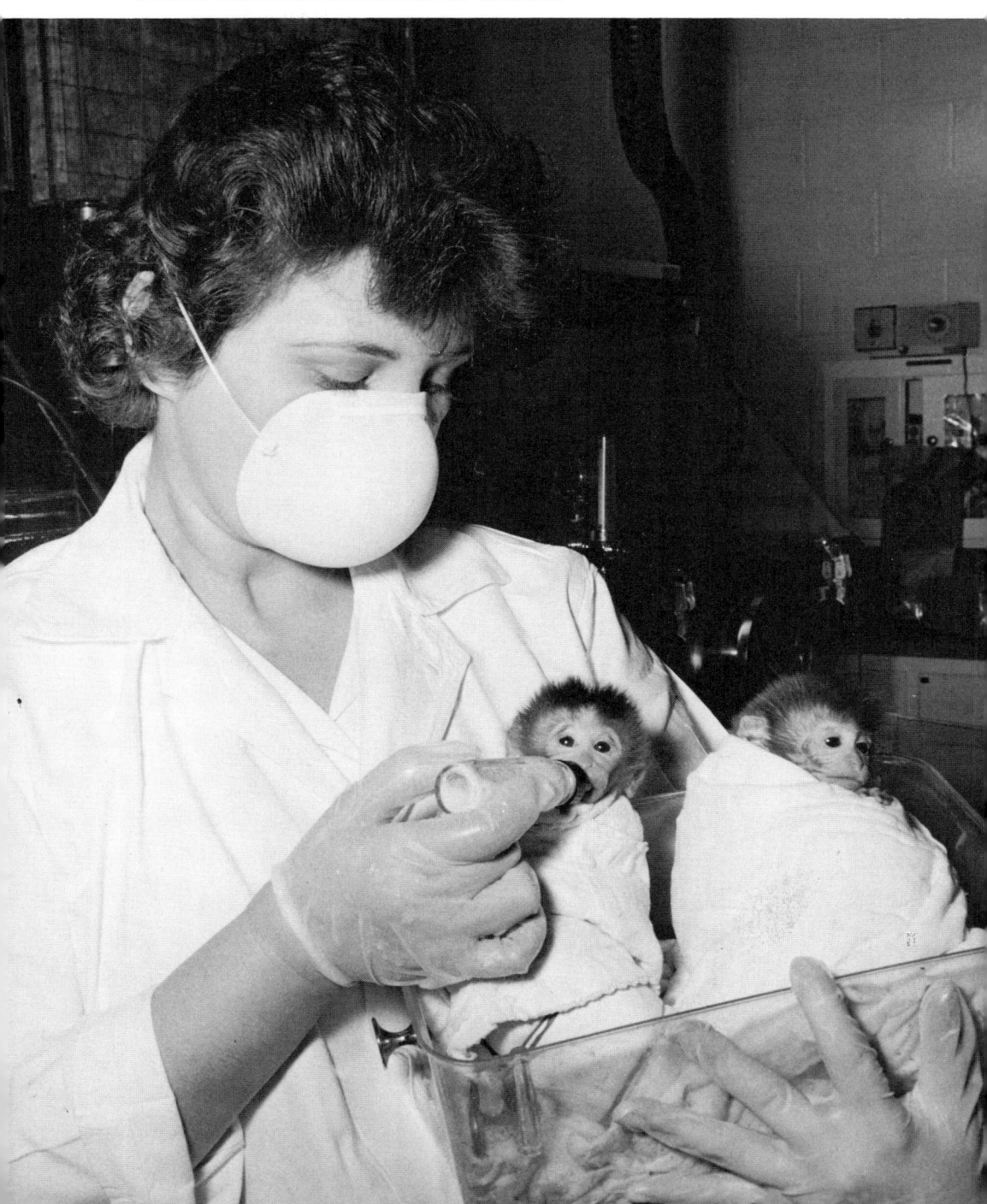

may help other scientists to develop a tobacco leaf which does not produce these cancer-causing chemicals. Perhaps they will make a filter that will remove the chemicals from cigarette smoke.

Cancer scientists are also studying radiation which is used as a cancer treatment, but can also cause cancer. Scientists expose lab animals to radiation from X rays and other sources. They observe the animals closely. They find that radiation causes an increased number of cases of leukemia, a type of cancer.

The statisticians have learned that sunlight, which is a type of radiation, is another cause of cancer. Farmers, fishermen and others who work outdoors in bright sunlight have cancer of the skin more often than other people. Also, people who live in the sunny southern and western parts of the United States develop more skin cancers than people who live in other parts of the country.

The scientists who study the effect of radiation want to know: How does radiation change normal cells into cancer cells? Is there a "safe" level of radiation? Is there a protection against radiation?

Dr. Frank J. Rauscher, Director of the National Cancer Institute, is a leading cancer scientist. He sums up the basic purpose of research into the causes of cancer this way: "At least eighty-five percent of our cancers are due to something that we do. And if that's true, we ought to be able to prevent it."

Cancer-cause research is the necessary first step toward cancer prevention.

THE VIROLOGISTS

Virologists are scientists who study viruses. The difficulties in their research are staggering!

The viruses are so tiny that they can only be separated from other material by using a filter with holes so small that not even a single cell can pass through. The viruses are so tiny, in fact, that they cannot be seen through an ordinary microscope.

At times the viruses are lifeless chemicals that can be kept in glass jars. But, when these same viruses are placed near living cells, they spring into life, growing and multiplying like other living things.

At least twelve different kinds of animal cancers are

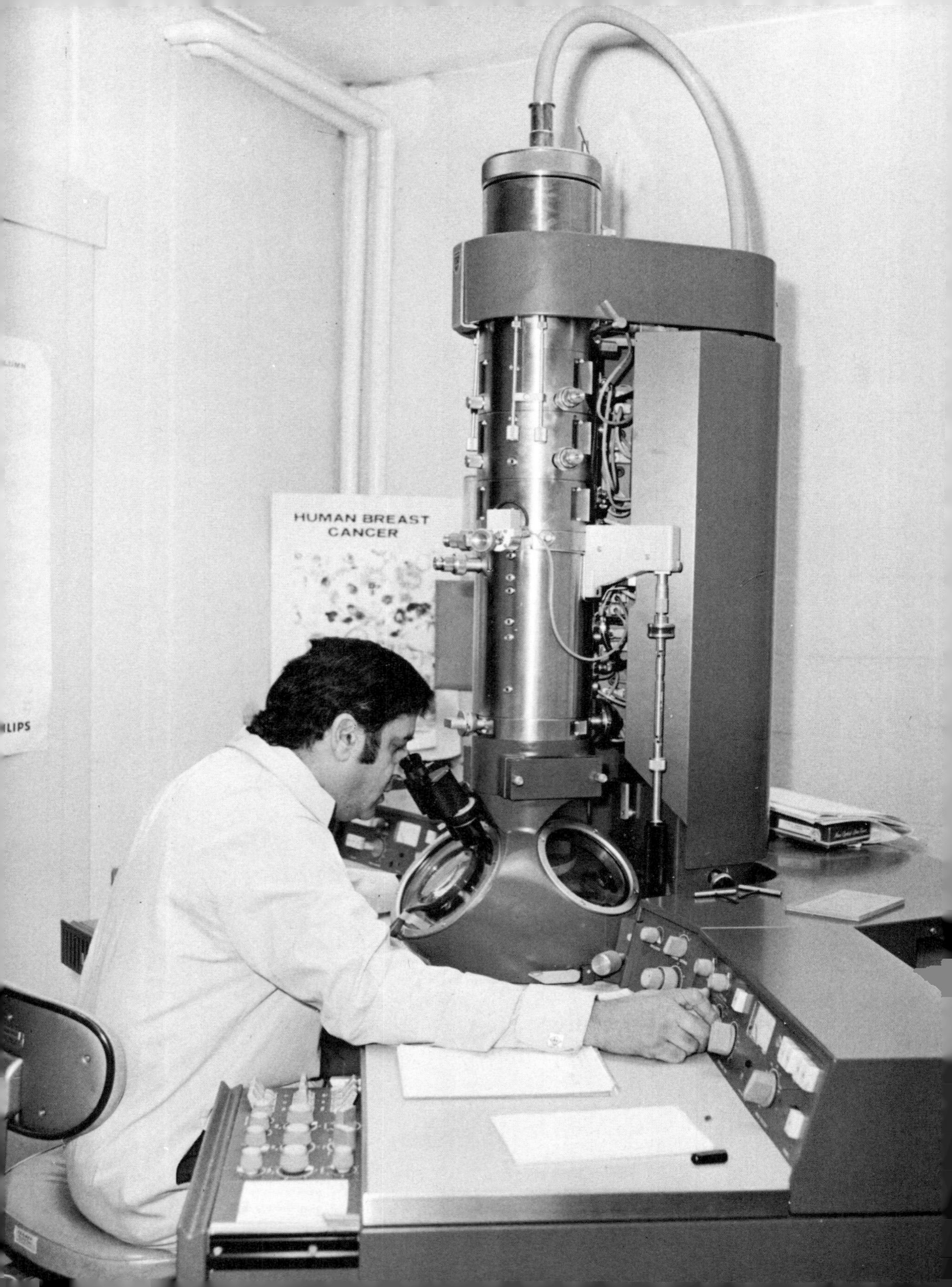
HUMAN BREAST
CANCER

known to be caused by viruses. Until now, though, no one has been able to prove that human cancer is virus-caused.

The viruses that cause most diseases destroy the cells that they attack. Cancer-causing viruses, however, make cells grow wildly and divide without stop.

A well-known virus researcher at the National Cancer Institute, Dr. John B. Moloney, says: "The only sane cancer virus researchers are those either with holes in their heads, or holes in their filters!"

To prove that a virus causes human cancer, virologists must follow this basic plan: They must be able to find the virus in cancer cells. They must then use the virus to grow more viruses. And finally, they must use the new viruses to cause cancer in other cells.

The virologists have several amazing instruments and methods to help carry out this important research.

To separate the viruses from the cells with which they are mixed, the virologists use the ultracentrifuge. This modern tool is an advance on the centrifuge used in the clinical lab. It spins the mixture around at speeds as high as 60,000 revolutions per minute. By adjusting the speed and the length of time the mixture is spun, the virologists are able to remove the pure viruses from the mixture.

To see the viruses, the virologists use an electron microscope. In the usual microscope, light passes through a specimen and through several glass lenses. The specimen then appears up to 2,500 times its actual size. In the electron microscope, a stream of electrons passes through the specimen and past several magnets. The specimen then appears up to 200,000 times its actual size.

The virologists usually grow the viruses on living cells

The electron microscope looks entirely different from an ordinary microscope. It is the only way the virologist is able to see the viruses. PHOTO: NATIONAL CANCER INSTITUTE

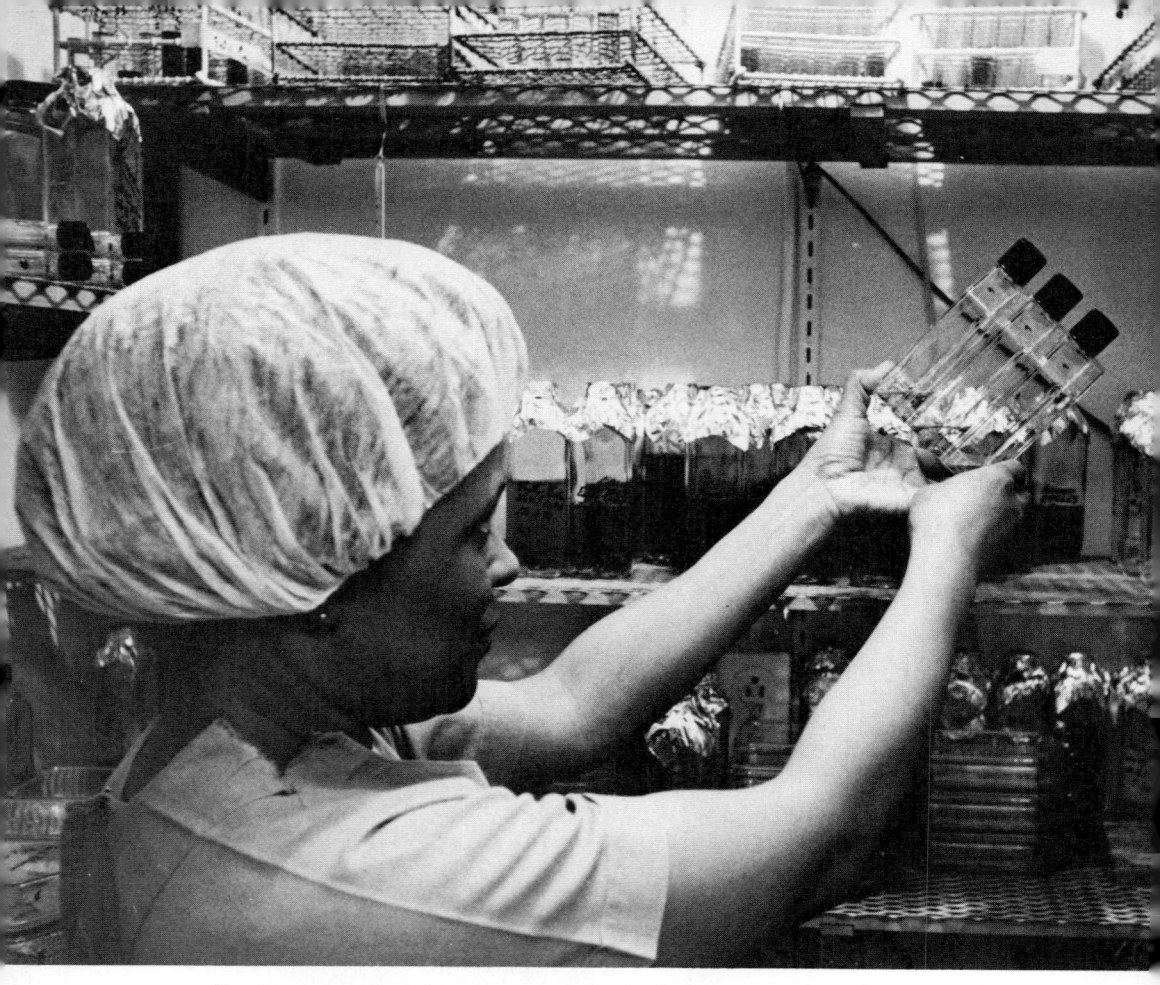

Each of the bottles the scientist is holding, and each of the flasks and test tubes on the shelf, contains cells growing in a liquid medium. PHOTO: NATIONAL INSTITUTES OF HEALTH

in a test tube. This method of growing cells is known as cell culture or tissue culture.

Technicians in the virology lab place some living cells and a medium in a flask or test tube. The cells are either special strains of cells grown for laboratory experiments, or cells taken from a cancer patient or lab animal. The medium is either blood plasma or a mixture of chemicals on which cells can live. The cells grow and multiply in the medium.

The viruses are added to the cell culture. The viruses reproduce and increase in quantity. They behave just as they do in a living being. Virologists then use this supply of new viruses to carry on their research.

Part of virus research is in the lab. Part is at a desk and blackboard. This photo shows Dr. John B. Moloney, a leading virologist, at work at his desk. PHOTO: NATIONAL CANCER INSTITUTE

The virologists inject the new viruses into different lab animals, from mice to monkeys, to find out whether they will cause cancer. They are given at different points in the animals' life cycles. Sometimes they are mixed with other viruses and chemicals.

In spite of the difficulties of cancer-virus research, scientists are learning a lot. And they are finding ways to prevent and control virus-caused cancers—even before the role of viruses in the body is fully understood.

Dr. John B. Moloney is a leading virologist. Some years ago he discovered a virus that caused leukemia in mice. It is known as the Moloney virus.

Researchers at the National Cancer Institute are working to develop an anticancer vaccine from the Moloney and other leukemia-causing viruses. The viruses are either killed or weakened.

The scientists inject some of these viruses into healthy mice. Each mouse produces antibodies which protect it against the virus. The antibodies remain in its blood. Later, when the experimenters inject living viruses into the mice, they find that the antibodies attack the viruses. These mice do not develop leukemia. In fact, these mice do not develop other types of cancer, either.

Some virologists at the National Cancer Institute are injecting parts of living viruses into goats. The goats develop antibodies. The antibodies are separated from the goats' blood, and made into a vaccine. The vaccine is used to protect other goats from attack by the whole virus.

The virologists want to master the ways to prepare an anticancer vaccine for animals. Then, if a virus is found that causes a human cancer, they will be better able to make an anticancer vaccine for humans.

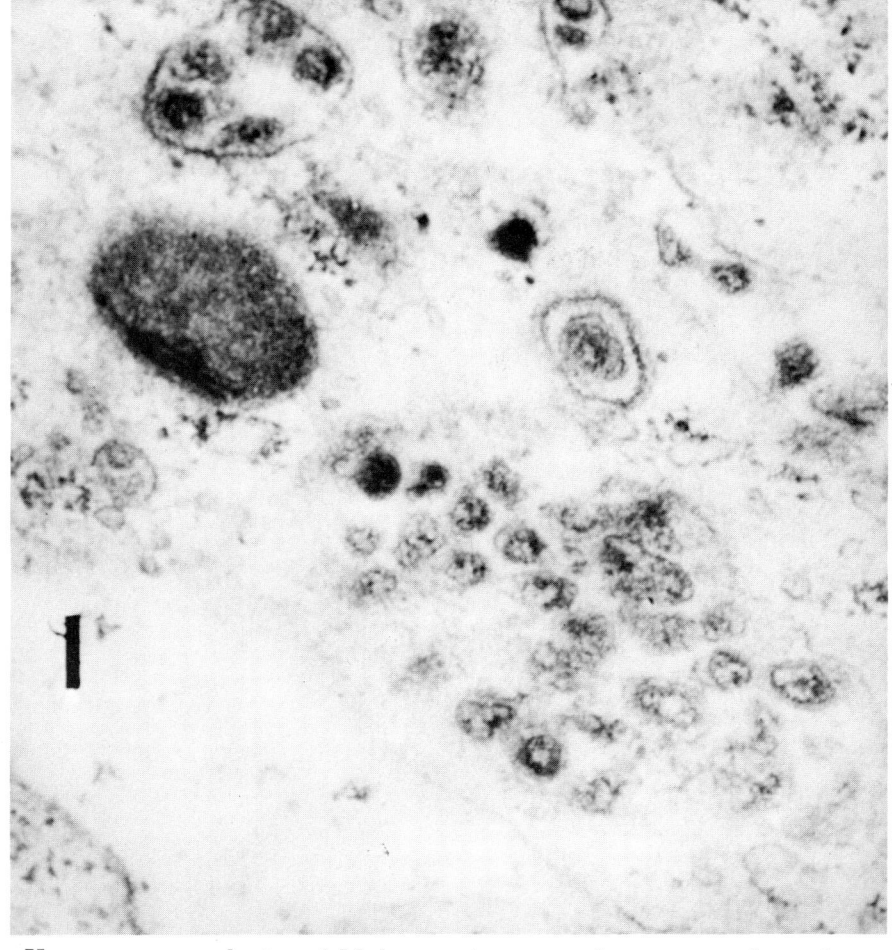

Here you see a cluster of Moloney viruses as they appear through an electron microscope. They are the dark particles in the lower half of the picture. PHOTO: NATIONAL CANCER INSTITUTE

Dr. Albert B. Sabin is one of the most famous virologists of our time. In 1961, he developed a vaccine for the virus-caused disease, polio. His vaccine helped to eliminate polio as a health problem. Since 1963, Dr. Sabin has been working in cancer-virus research.

Famous for his discovery of the polio virus vaccine, Dr. Albert B. Sabin is now doing research on the connection between viruses and cancer. PHOTO: NATIONAL CANCER INSTITUTE

Currently, Dr. Sabin is studying a very common type of virus, called *herpes simplex*. This causes the blisters or sores that sometimes appear on the lips after a bad cold. Almost everyone has been infected by the *herpes simplex* virus at one time or another.

Dr. Sabin has been able to show a statistical link between this virus and nine types of human cancer. In examining the blood of people suffering from these nine cancers, he finds antibodies directed against the *herpes simplex* virus. Yet, he cannot find these antibodies in the blood of people who have had the virus infections, but not cancer.

It seems that the antibodies are somehow part of the process of cancer development. The *herpes simplex* virus, along with other factors, plays some role in causing cancer. His studies on the antibodies in cancer patients may bring scientists closer yet to solving the cancer-virus puzzle.

About three out of every five virologists are working on human cancers. They are looking for evidence of viruses in cancer tissue, preparing vaccines from cancer cells in an effort to trace how cancer viruses might be transmitted from person to person.

Right now, the virologists have as many questions on cancer-virus links as they have answers. But as long as they keep asking the right questions, they will keep moving ahead.

DRUG SCREENERS

Cancer research for Dr. Robert E. Perdue is filled with many adventures. Spear-carrying Masai tribesmen visit his truck and trailer near the Ngong Hills, in Kenya, Africa. He climbs the Pink Cliffs of Utah. He visits the open-air market in Addis Ababa, Ethiopia. He talks about medicinal plants with a woman in tribal dress at Kekonyokie, Kenya.

Dr. Perdue is a botanist. He is trained in the science of plants. His role in cancer research is to collect plants from all over the world. Other cancer researchers then test these plants to see if any can be used as drugs to fight cancer.

Every year, Dr. Perdue and other scientists in the field

collect about 5,000 plant samples. Some they choose just because they have not been tested before. Others are plants that they set out to collect. Among these are plants related to the ones that are known to produce cancer drugs. There are also plants that the scientists think may be effective, and plants believed to have curing powers by the people in the area.

Spear-carrying Masai tribesmen visit Dr. Robert E. Perdue's truck and trailer while he is collecting plants near the Ngong Hills in East Africa. PHOTO: U.S. DEPARTMENT OF AGRICULTURE

Dr. Perdue always brings back any untested plants related to the periwinkle shrub, for example. *Vincristine,* a very successful cancer drug, is made from the plant. Perhaps similar plants might contain other cancer drugs.

On the other hand, he no longer collects plants related to the daisy. Daisylike plants have not shown any activity against cancer.

But finding the plants is only part of Dr. Perdue's work. He must collect enough to allow the scientists back in the labs to do the necessary tests. He must separate and dry various parts of the plant—leaves, flowers, stem, root, bark and seeds. And he must keep careful records on each type of plant, including where and when he found it. This information is most important for further testing and for later production of the drug if it should prove successful. He then ships the plant samples back to the drug-screening lab.

Let us say that Dr. Perdue sends back a sample of leaves from Tanzania in East Africa. Chemists in the lab grind up the leaves. They add alcohol and water to remove, or extract, all the chemicals that might be in the leaves. Finally, they evaporate the water and alcohol, leaving only the chemicals. These chemicals make up the drug that will be tested to see if it works against cancer cells.

In another part of the lab, scientists grow the mice that are used in the drug-screening experiments. These mice are bred to produce a pure strain. They will all react in the same way to the drug.

The researchers inject a particular type of cancer cells into a group of perhaps six mice. They know that these

The truck is loaded down with plants that were collected in the Pink Cliffs of Utah. PHOTO: U.S. DEPARTMENT OF AGRICULTURE

cells will grow and cause cancer in the mice. They also know that an untreated mouse will die within ten days.

Then they inject the test drug into the mice. Nothing happens to any of the mice during the first nine days of the experiment. On the tenth day, one mouse dies. On the eleventh day another one dies. The remaining four last until the thirteenth day.

The results show that the leaf might contain a cancer drug. The scientists decide to repeat the experiment. They receive about the same results. They decide to continue the testing program. They call on Dr. Perdue to arrange for another shipment of these leaves to the lab.

It is up to the lab chemists to find all of the separate chemicals in the leaves. They put the plant material through a series of chemical operations. Each one divides the material into separate chemical compounds, called fractions. At the end, the chemists have five different fractions.

The fractions go back to the researchers who work with the mice. They test each fraction in a new group of mice that have been injected with cancer cells. They find the fraction that works best against the mouse cancer.

The active fraction then goes back to the chemists. They break it down into smaller fractions. These very small fractions are tested on more mice. Finally, the chemists find the purest, simplest compound that works against the cancer. This is the cancer drug.

To learn more about the drugs, the researchers plan further experiments. Each experiment answers a question, such as: What happens to the drug in the body of the mouse? Does the drug have any side effects? How

The open-air market in Addis Ababa, Ethiopia, is an excellent source of medicinal plants.
PHOTO: U.S. DEPARTMENT OF AGRICULTURE

Dr. Perdue learns about medicinal plants by talking to people who live in the area. Here he discusses some plants with a woman in tribal dress at Kekonyokie, Kenya.
PHOTO: U.S. DEPARTMENT OF AGRICULTURE

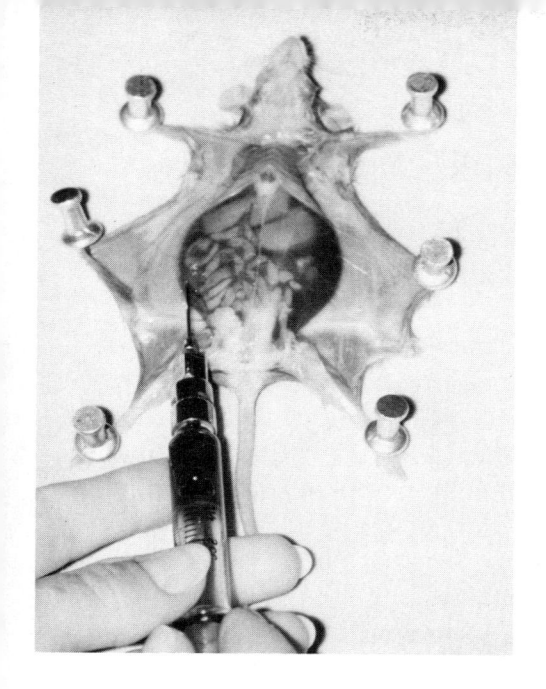

This mouse died of leukemia. The researcher is removing some leukemia cells to inject into a healthy mouse as part of the drug-screening research.
PHOTO: U.S. DEPARTMENT OF AGRICULTURE

much of the drug is needed to control the cancer? How much of the drug will poison the mouse?

Similar tests and experiments are also repeated on larger animals, such as dogs and monkeys. If the drug passes all the tests, it is ready to be tested on humans.

Physicians choose patients who have had all the known treatments for cancer, and yet are close to death from the disease. The patients are all volunteers who understand the experiment, and agree to take part. To learn if the drug is poisonous, or toxic, they give the patients small doses of the new drug. Gradually they give larger and larger doses.

The physicians also test the best way to give the drug—pill, liquid or injection. It takes two years to collect all the information from these tests.

If the results are good, the drug is ready to be tested on a large number of patients. Several hundred patients are needed. They are divided into groups of patients that have the same types of cancer, and are at the same stage of the disease. Some people in each group receive the new drug; some do not. The condition of the cancer and general health of each person who receives the drug is compared to those who do not receive it.

It takes a few more years for the results to come in. As much as researchers want to discover new cancer drugs, they are very careful not to release any drug that might be harmful.

There are other scientists in the drug-screening program who collect nonplant chemicals to be tested as cancer drugs. The chemicals are put through the same tests as the plants. In fact, more chemicals than plant products have been made into anticancer drugs.

Over the years only a small number of successful drugs have been found among the many thousands of plants and chemicals that have been tested. Each year, though, the list of cancer drugs does grow longer. In 1968 the National Cancer Institute listed twenty-six cancer drugs. Five years later, the same list included forty-four cancer drugs. And we can be sure that future lists will include even more new and better cancer drugs.

BASIC CANCER RESEARCHERS

There are many cancer researchers who never see a cancer patient. They have nothing to do with cancer treatments. They do not search for the causes of cancer. These scientists are in basic cancer research. They work to learn more about the biology of cancer.

Dr. Raymond Gesteland is a well-known scientist doing basic cancer research at the Cold Spring Harbor Laboratory on Long Island, New York. He is not a medical doctor and his field of research is a very narrow one. He is trying to find out exactly what happens when an animal-cancer virus attacks a living cell. He is particularly interested in discovering how the viruses manufacture one part—the protein—of the new viruses that appear.

Dr. Raymond Gesteland of the Cold Spring Harbor Laboratory carefully collects exactly ten drops in each glass tube. In this way he is able to separate the parts of a mixture by weight after using the sucrose gradient. PHOTO: MELVIN BERGER

If Dr. Gesteland were to announce the exact process of protein manufacture today, it probably would not change the methods of preventing, detecting and treating human cancer immediately.

But, in the long run, it would be of great help to other cancer researchers. Once the physicians know the basic biology of cancer cells, they can work to detect the disease earlier and treat it better. Once the chemotherapists and immunologists know what is special about cancer cells, they can narrow their search for ways to destroy these cells. And, once the virologists know how the viruses work in a cell, they will be better able to prepare vaccines to protect against any human cancer viruses that might be found.

In his day-to-day work, Dr. Gesteland uses many of the methods and tools you have already read about. He uses the ultracentrifuge, for example, many times a day. This tool separates out the proteins from the mixture of cell material, viruses and medium which he obtains from tissue culture.

Dr. Gesteland adds the mixture to a tube filled with dissolved sugar, called a sucrose gradient. The gradient is heaviest and thickest at the bottom. It grows lighter and thinner toward the top. He uses the sucrose gradient to separate out the parts of the mixtures by weights.

Dr. Gesteland places the mixture on the top surface of the sucrose gradient. He then places it in the ultracentrifuge and spins it around. The different parts of the mixture move down through the sucrose gradient. The heaviest parts move fastest and farthest. The lighter parts move the least. When the tube is removed from the ultracentrifuge, the different parts of the original mixture are found in bands at various heights in the tube.

To separate out the different parts, Dr. Gesteland allows the contents of the tube to drip out through a tiny opening in the bottom. He collects exactly ten drops each

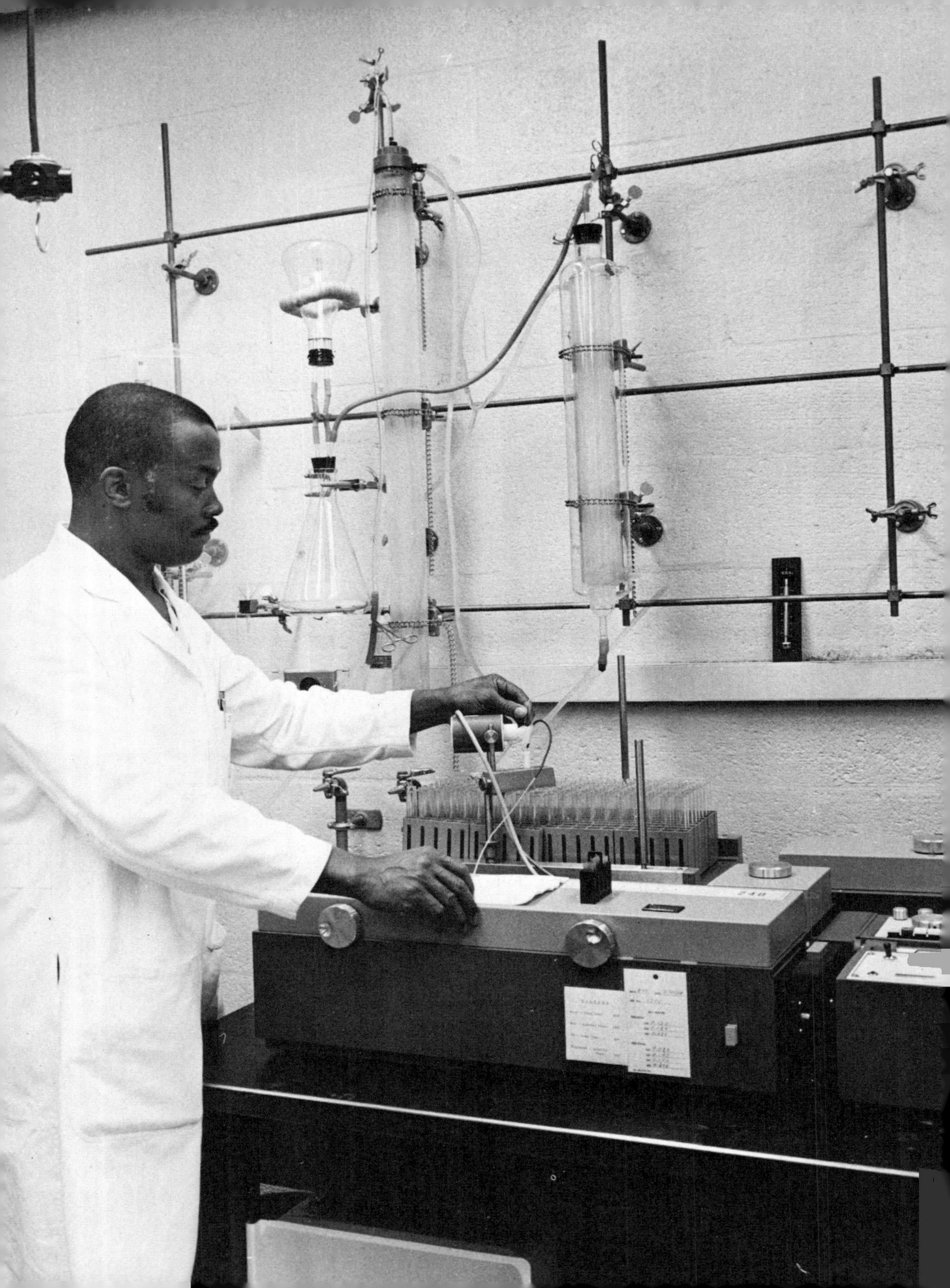

in many small glass containers. The first ten drops contain the heaviest sucrose; therefore, it also contains the heaviest part of the mixture. Each of the following containers holds lighter and lighter parts of the mixture with which he began.

Scientists do not only separate the parts of a mixture by weight. They also use a method known as chromatography.

The scientist places the substance to be analyzed on top of a hollow column packed with a material, such as powdered chalk, charcoal or any one of about a dozen other materials. Next, the scientist adds a liquid that dissolves the original substance. This solvent washes the parts of the substance down the column. The parts that are least attracted to the packing material go farthest and fastest. Those that are more attracted by the material remain up near the top of the column.

There is a tiny hole at the bottom of the column. If more solvent is added, the various parts drip out at different times. By collecting just a few drops, in separate containers, the parts are separated.

Dr. Gesteland guesses that basic cancer researchers use radioisotopes in about 95 percent of their experiments. Radioisotopes, as mentioned earlier, send out atomic radiation. They are the same as ordinary elements in all other ways.

Suppose a scientist wants to trace and measure the amount of calcium in various cells. The cells are placed in a medium containing a radioisotope of calcium so that they take in some of the chemical. The various parts of the cell are then separated into individual containers.

The scientist places a mixture at the top of one of the chromatography columns. He collects the individual chemicals in the racks of tubes under his left hand. PHOTO: NATIONAL INSTITUTES OF HEALTH

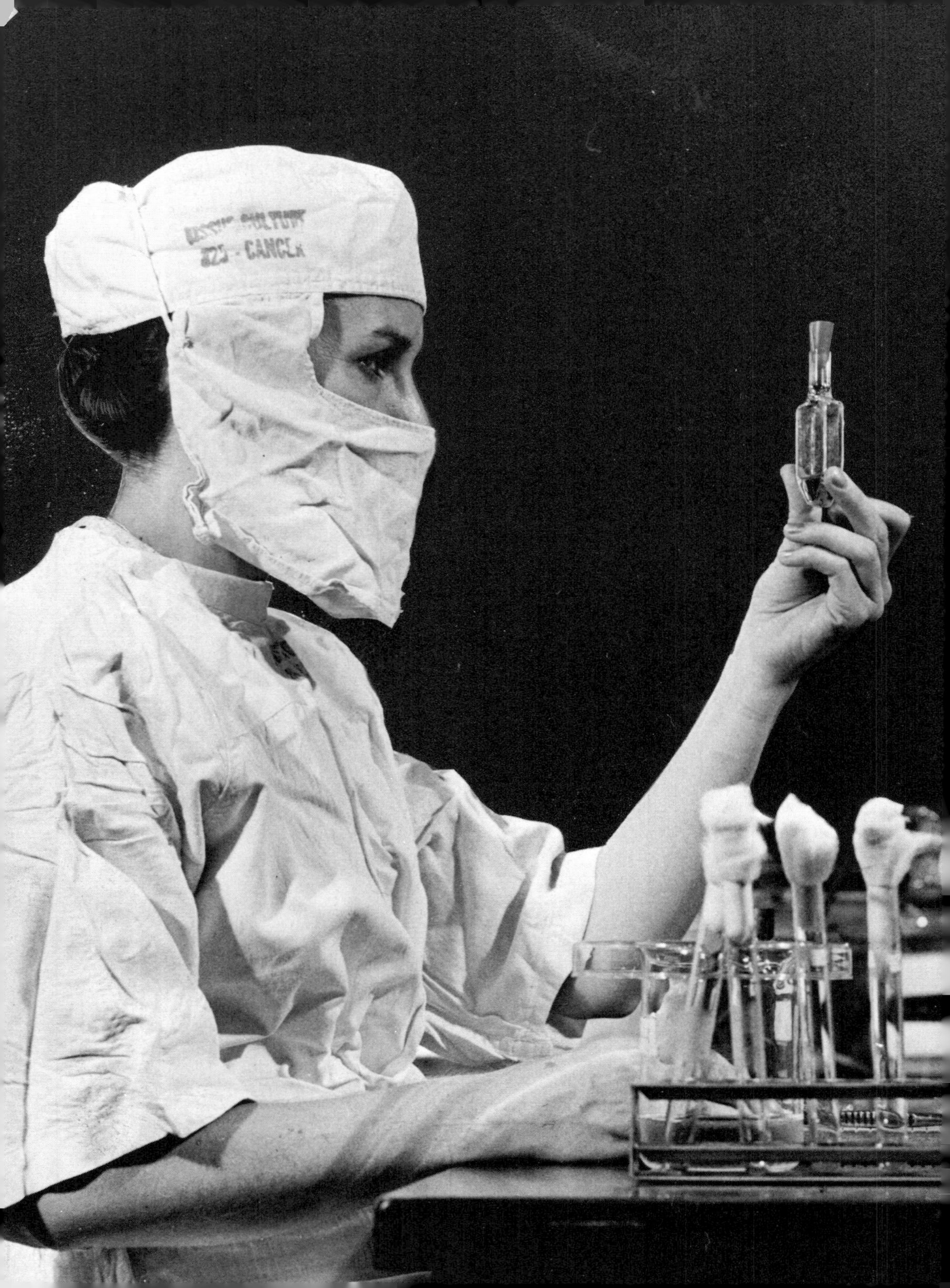

These technicians are growing cells in the test tubes. They wear masks and gowns, so there is no danger of their germs getting into the cells. PHOTO: NATIONAL CANCER INSTITUTE

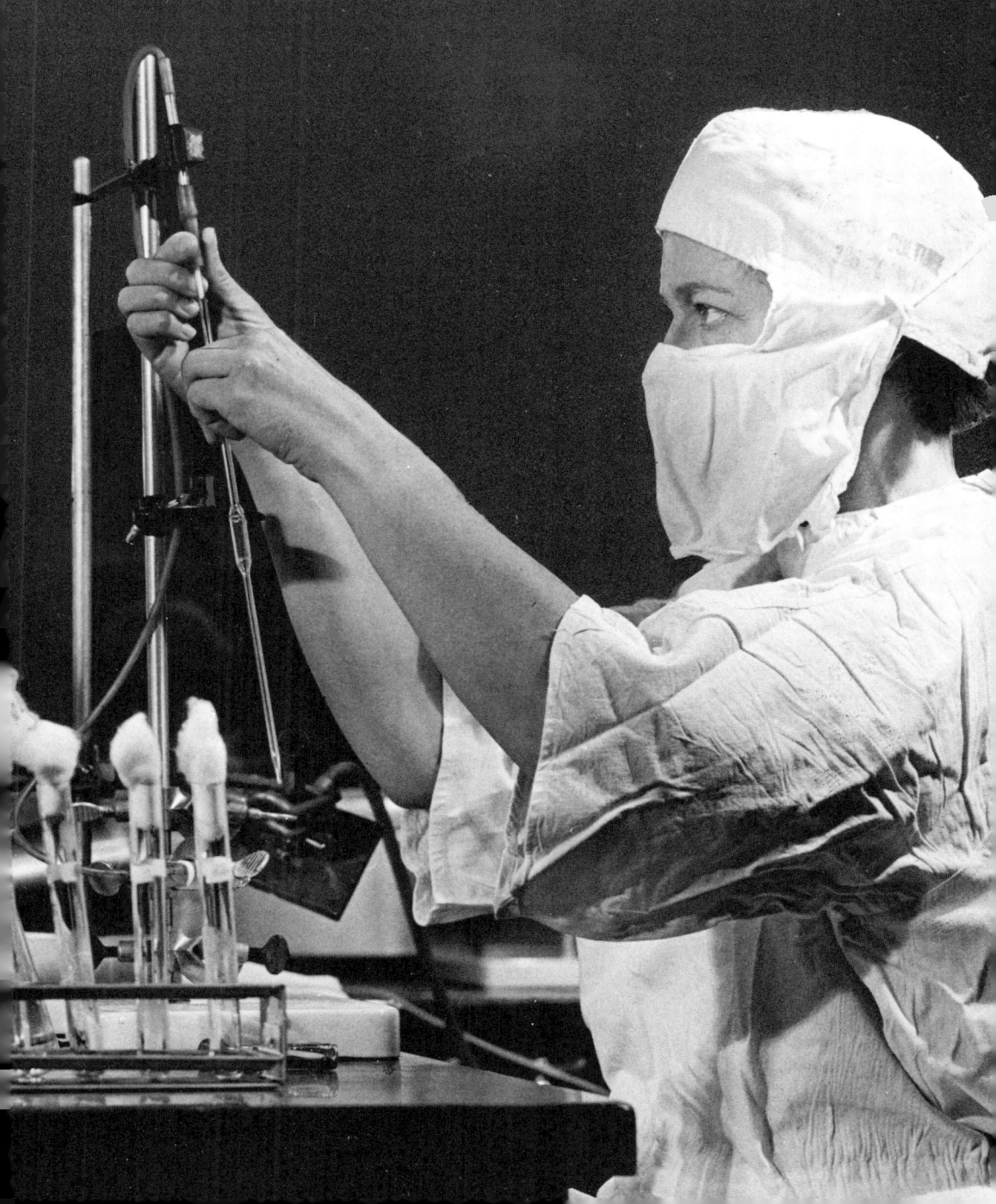

Most research is based on the work of others. This scientist reads a report that might help her plan her experiment.
PHOTO: NATIONAL INSTITUTES OF HEALTH

Each container of the separated sample is placed in a scintillation counter. The scintillation counter measures the radiation given off by the radioisotope of calcium. Each container is exposed separately. The more radiation, the more of the radioisotope of calcium is present in those cells.

Most of the time, scientists and technicians in a basic research lab work at lab benches. They use the various tools of modern biology. They handle test tubes and flasks filled with different kinds of liquids. They are busy with the bread-and-butter tasks that are part of all experiments.

But the most important work does not take place then. It takes place when it looks as though nothing at all is happening in the lab.

Scientific discoveries do not only come when the researcher is hard at work at the lab bench. New theories are often born as two researchers chat in the lab. PHOTO: NATIONAL INSTITUTES OF HEALTH

New theories may be born as scientists are talking over a cup of coffee. Or, new directions for research may be struck as a scientist sits staring out of the window in the evening when everyone else has gone home. Someone else reading a book and making notes on a pad may hit on an idea that will lead to an important discovery.

Breakthroughs in basic research come very rarely. But there is good reason to celebrate each one, when it happens.

These happy moments are coming more and more often in the labs of the basic cancer researchers. They are making discoveries that add more information about how the human body works. They are finding new facts and figures and understandings to pass along to the other cancer researchers.

The scientists in basic research are most hopeful. They know that their work, and the work of the scientists who apply today's research to patients, is bringing us ever closer to victory in the war against cancer.

FURTHER READING

Berger, Melvin, *Tools of Modern Biology*, New York, T.Y. Crowell Co., 1970.
Boesch, Mark, *The Long Search for the Truth About Cancer*, New York, G. P. Putnam's, 1960.
Brooke, Bryan N., *Understanding Cancer*, New York, Holt, Rinehart and Winston, 1971
Brooks, Stewart M., *The Cancer Story*, Cranbury, N.J., A. S. Barnes, 1973
Glemser, Bernard, *Man Against Cancer*, New York, Funk & Wagnalls, 1969
Prescott, David, *Cancer: The Misguided Cell*, Indianapolis, Bobbs-Merrill, 1973

Silverstein, Alvin and Virginia, *Cancer*, New York, John Day, 1972

Write to these addresses for free booklets and other material on cancer:

American Cancer Society
219 East 42nd Street
New York, N.Y. 10017

Canadian Cancer Society
Davisville Street
Toronto, Canada

National Cancer Institute
National Institutes of Health
Bethesda, Maryland 20014

INDEX

American Cancer Society, 91
Antibodies, 55, 58, 59, 100, 103
"Atomic cocktail," 28
Autoanalyzer, 67, 69
Autotechnicon, 81

Bacillus Calmette-Guérin. *See* BCG
Barium, 25
BCG, 58-59, 64
Betatron, 37, 44
Biochemist, 73, 74
Biopsy, 29, 75, 76, 79
Blocking factor, 61, 64
Breast cancer, 50, 51, 52

Cancer
   breast, 50, 51, 52
   causes, 19, 85-94, 95-97
   cells, 15, 19, 28, 30, 31, 36, 44, 45, 48, 52, 53-54, 59, 61, 64, 69, 103, 115
   cure, 15
   detection, 15, 20-28, 73, 115
   as disease, 13, 14
   drugs, 46-52, 104-12
   lung, 13, 23, 91-94
   ovary, 50
   and radiation, 94
   skin, 13, 61, 94
   and smoking, 89-94
   stomach, 13, 25
   and sunlight, 94
   treatment, 19, 31, 32-34, 35-45, 46-52, 53-64, 65-66, 73
   uterus, 22
   and X rays, 94

Canellos, Dr. George P., 46, 50, 51-52
Cell culture, 97-99
Cell poison, 48
Cells, 15, 19, 22, 23, 36, 48, 75, 77, 97-99, 113, 115, 117, 120
Centrifuge, 67
Chemotherapist, 46-52
Chemotherapy, 46-52, 64, 115
Chromatography, 117
Clinical laboratory, 65-74
Cobalt-60, 37-40
Cold Spring Harbor Laboratory, 113
Computer, 35, 67, 69
Cryosurgery, 34
Cyclotron, 44

Deblocking factor, 61, 64
De Vita, Dr. Vincent T., 50

Electron microscope, 97
Electrons, 37, 44

Fisher, Dr. Richard, 53, 58, 59
Fleischer, Dr. Martin, 74

Gamma rays, 36, 37, 40, 44
Gesteland, Dr. Raymond, 113-17
Goat, 100
Gross examination, 80, 83

Heaf gun, 53, 59
Hellstrom, Drs. Karl and Ingegord, 60-61
Herpes simplex, 103
High-energy X rays, 37
Hodgkin's disease, 37, 50
Hormones, 48, 50

Immune system, 55, 58, 61, 64, 115
Immunologists, 53-64

Jenner, Dr. Edward, 55

Leukemia, 48, 94, 100
Linear accelerator, 37
Lung cancer, 13, 23, 91-94

Mathé, Dr. Georges, 58
Melanoma, 61
Memorial Sloan-Kettering Cancer Center, 66, 73, 74
Mice, 85, 87-89, 91-94, 100, 106-108
Microscope, 30, 75, 77, 80, 95, 97
Microtome, 77, 83
Moloney, Dr. John B., 87, 100

National Cancer Institute, 46, 50, 53, 58, 91, 94, 97, 100, 112
NCI. *See* National Cancer Institute

Operation. *See* Surgery
Organ transplant, 32, 34
Ovary cancer, 50
Oxygen, 44

Pap test, 22
Papanicolaou, Dr. George. *See* Pap test
Pathologists, 75-84
Pathology lab, 76, 79, 80, 83, 84
Perdue, Dr. Robert E., 104-6, 108

Physician, 20-28, 29, 31-32, 34, 35, 40, 45, 59, 65, 69, 70, 73, 80, 83, 115
Protons, 44

Radiation, 35-45, 52, 117, 120
Radioisotopes, 28, 117, 120
Radiotherapist, 35-45
Radiotherapy, 35-45, 50
Rauscher, Dr. Frank J., 94
Reagent, 67
Robinson, Dr. Joseph, 64

Sabin, Dr. Albert B., 101-3
Scanner, 28
Scintillation counter, 120
Skin cancer, 13, 61, 94
Smallpox, 55
Statistician, 90-91, 94
Stomach cancer, 13, 25
Sucrose gradient, 115-17

Surgeon, 29-34, 37, 75
Surgery, 31-34, 37, 52

Tissue culture, 97-99
Tuberculosis, 58
Tumors, benign, 22, 31
Tumors, malignant, 22

Ultracentrifuge, 97, 115
Uterus cancer, 22

Vaccination, 55-58
Vaccine, 55, 58, 59, 100, 101, 103, 115
Virologists, 95-103
Viruses, 19, 55, 58, 95-103, 113, 115

X-ray machine, 37, 40, 44
X rays, 23-25, 36, 37, 40, 44, 94

SCIENTISTS AT WORK